FIRST GRADE

Smart Start

This book belongs to

colby

_____
Name

Cover Design: Carrie Duncan
Cover Illustration: Olga1818/
              Shutterstock.com
Illustration: Mary Rojas
              (pages 15–19, 22–24,40–44,
              73–77, 83–89)
Art Direction: Yuki Meyer
Design/Production: Yuki Meyer

EMC 9849

Evan-Moor®
Helping Children Learn

**Congratulations on your
purchase of some of the
finest teaching materials
in the world.**

For information about other Evan-Moor products, call 1-800-777-4362,
fax 1-800-777-4332, or visit our website, www.evan-moor.com.
Entire contents © 2017 EVAN-MOOR CORP.
18 Lower Ragsdale Drive, Monterey, CA 93940-5746. Printed in China.

CPSIA: Super Step Productions, Tsuen Wan, Hong Kong [1/2017]

Dear Parents,

Children have a natural instinct to learn and succeed when they enjoy what they are doing. The activities in this book are designed to provide your child with a fun way to learn the basic skills and concepts he or she needs to succeed in school and in life. Supporting your child's learning experiences can help your child develop a love of learning.

Research shows that the skills below are fundamental to developing literacy skills in reading, math, science, and geography.

- phonemic awareness, phonics, fluency
- vocabulary, comprehension
- number sense, geometry
- algebra
- measurement
- map skills, basic geography concepts
- life science concepts, physical science concepts

We hope you and your child will enjoy working together to complete the activities in this book. Learning is fun and you are your child's best teacher!

Sincerely,
Evan-Moor Educational Publishers
Helping Children Learn since 1979

Get a Smart Start!

Provide a Quiet Place
Find a quiet place for your child to work. Make this a special time for you and your child to spend together learning new things.

Encourage and Support
Your response is important to your child's feelings of success. Keep your remarks positive and recognize the effort your child has made. Correct mistakes together. Work toward independence, guiding practice when necessary.

Build Reading Comprehension

Listen as your child reads to you. Help your child sound out or identify any words he or she does not know. Discuss word meaning. Encourage your child to talk about how the pictures and illustrations give clues about the words on the page.

Connect Learning to the Real World

As your child completes the activities in this book, help him or her make connections to the real world. If the theme is monkeys, talk about real-life monkeys. Allow your child to express his or her own thoughts and ideas and to ask you questions. Help your child understand that learning reading, math, science, geography, and critical thinking skills will help him or her better understand the world we live in.

Timing Is Important

Consider your child's personality and other activities as you decide how and where to schedule practice periods. The practice sessions should be short and positive.

Make Learning Fun!

Reading Contents

Math Contents

Science Contents

Geography Contents

Thinking Skills Contents

Art Contents

Reading Foundations and Comprehension

Helping Your Child with Reading Foundations and Comprehension

When children learn to read, they are decoding words using phonics skills and making sense of what they say. They also use reading comprehension skills. The stories and activites in this section provide practice with both of these fundamental skills. In addition, a variety of activities engage children in tasks such as giving their opinion, using prior knowledge, solving problems, and determining word meaning.

Short Stories

The short stories and meaningful illustrations provide your child with a variety of simple stories to read. Support your child as he or she reads, providing assistance when needed. Discuss the illustrations with your child and talk about how they provide clues about the story. Point out that the pictures provide more information about the characters and the setting.

Reading Comprehension Activities

Each story is followed by comprehension activities that help your child think about what he or she read. Reading comprehension skills practiced include understanding word meaning, using picture clues, drawing conclusions, sequencing, categorizing, and more. Provide your child with support when needed as he or she completes the activities.

The Missing Mitten

One day Maria got ready to go outside. It was a cold, snowy day. Maria put on her snow pants. She put on her jacket. She put on her purple stocking hat. Her mother gave her a scarf to keep her neck warm. Next she pulled on her shiny purple snow boots. They were new. Maria couldn't wait to try them out. She was almost ready. All that she needed were her mittens.

73

Skills: Recalling Story Details; Understanding Opposites

What Did It Say?

Circle the words that tell about the cocoon and the sleeping bag.

cold   quiet   warm   bright

loud   busy   still   dark

Fill in the circle in front of the answer.

1. ○ It is warm here.
   ○ It is cold here.

2. ○ It is dark here.
   ○ It is bright here.

3. ○ It is loud here.
   ○ It is quiet here.

24

Smart Start • EMC 9849 • © Evan-Moor Corp.

Phonics Activities

The engaging phonics activities help your child practice important skills such as identifying beginning sounds, final sounds, vowel sounds, consonant blends, and word families. These activities also develop vocabulary skills and provide opportunities to apply words in context.

Drawing Activities

The drawing tasks provide children a creative way to demonstrate story comprehension, indicate word meaning, demonstrate understanding of a concept, or follow directions. Praise your child's drawing efforts and explain that drawing is another way to show what you know.

Certificate

After your child completes the reading section of this book, remove the reading certificate and have your child write his or her name on it. Congratulate your child on a job well done and post the certificate in a prominent place.

Dad and I

Dad rakes the lawn.

I rake the lawn, too!

Dad pulls the weeds.

I pull the weeds, too.

Dad washes the car.

I wash the car, too.

Dad takes a nap.

I take a nap, too.
Almost!

What Did It Say?

Mark the things that the girl and her dad did in the story.

- _X_ 1. They baked a cake.
- _✓_ 2. They raked the leaves.
- _X_ 3. They read a book.
- _✓_ 4. They pulled the weeds.
- _X_ 5. They washed the dog.
- _✓_ 6. They washed the car.

Draw something the dad did that the little girl did <u>not</u> do.

Before and After

Cut and paste to show how each thing looked before and after.

Before   **After**

The Lawn

| paste | We raked the leaves. | paste |

The Weeds

| paste | We pulled the weeds. | paste |

The Car

| paste | We washed the car. | paste |

The Sound of p

Circle the pictures that start with the sound **p** stands for.

key

pear

poodle

ball

penguin

purse

penny

cupcake

pizza

porcupine

pig

paint

Working with Word Families

ap

n + ap = __ __ __

c + ap = __ __ __

m + ap = __ __ __

scr + ap = __ __ __ __ __

tr + ap = __ __ __ __

str + ap = __ __ __ __ __

Read the word. Draw a line to the picture.

nap

strap

cap

map

My Cocoon

It's cold out there.

It's warm in here.

It's bright out there.

It's dark in here.

 Smart Start • EMC 9849 • © Evan-Moor Corp.

It's loud out there.

It's quiet in here.

It's busy out there.

It's still in here.

My sleeping bag is like a cocoon.

What Did It Say?

Circle the words that tell about the cocoon and the sleeping bag.

cold   quiet   warm   bright

loud   busy   still   dark

Fill in the circle in front of the answer.

1.
   - ○ It is warm here.
   - ○ It is cold here.

2.
   - ○ It is dark here.
   - ○ It is bright here.

3.
   - ○ It is loud here.
   - ○ It is quiet here.

Opposites

Words like **loud** and **quiet** are called opposites.
Draw a line to connect the opposites.

My hat is on.

up	clean
high	busy
bright	down
still	slow
fast	dark
dirty	low

My hat is off.

Draw pictures to show the opposites.

off

on

empty

full

Real or Make-Believe?

Circle **real** or **make-believe**.

real

make-believe

real

make-believe

real

make-believe

real

make-believe

Draw something about a butterfly that could be real.

Draw something about a butterfly that is make-believe.

Smart Start • EMC 9849 • © Evan-Moor Corp.

Put It in Order

Color, cut, and paste to put the pictures in order.
Write about each picture.

1

paste

_____

_____

_____

_____

2

paste

_____

_____

_____

_____

3

paste

_____

_____

_____

_____

Working with Word Families

h + ill = ___ ___ ___ ___

f + ill = ___ ___ ___ ___

ch + ill = ___ ___ ___ ___ ___

dr + ill = ___ ___ ___ ___ ___

Use the new words to complete these sentences.

1. Please _____ my glass with milk.

2. I need a _____ to fix the door.

3. He lives at the top of the _____.

4. If you go out in the cold, you will get

   a _____.

Finish the Picture

Draw the other side of the butterfly. Then color the picture.
Write about the butterfly.

My butterfly _____

_____

_____.

Who Can Fix It?

Smart Start • EMC 9849 • © Evan-Moor Corp.

What Did It Say?

Draw a picture of each thing.
Then draw lines to tell who fixed it.

button	wheel	knob

Mr. Snow   Sis   Uncle Joe

Which thing could <u>not</u> be fixed quickly?

button   wheel   knob   flower

Words That Rhyme

Write the four words in the story that rhyme with **know**.

_____   _____

_____   _____

The Same Sound

Color the pictures that begin with the same sound as button.

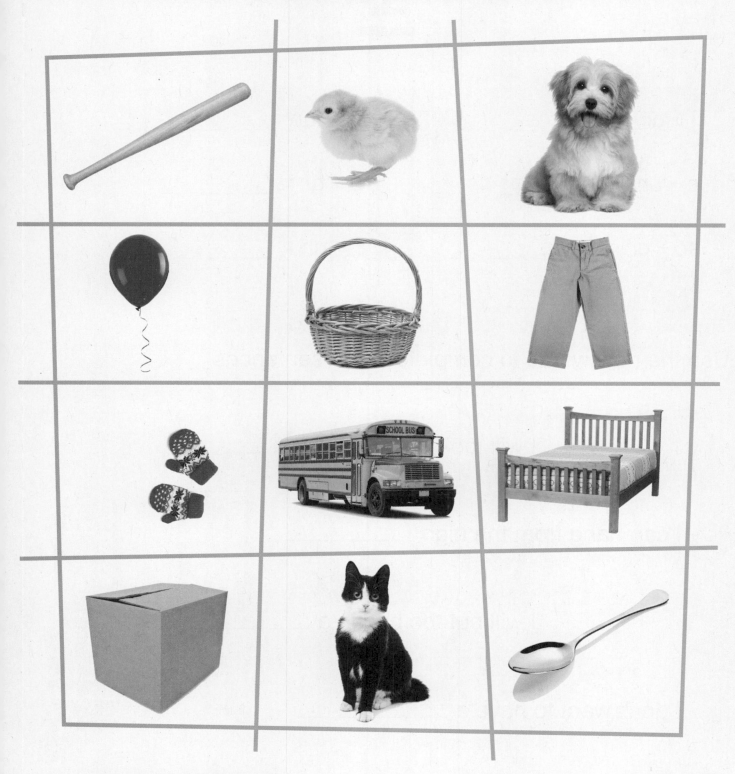

Working with Word Families

ar

j + ar = ___ ___ ___   st + ar = ___ ___ ___ ___

c + ar = ___ ___ ___   b + ar = ___ ___ ___

sc + ar = ___ ___ ___ ___   f + ar = ___ ___ ___

Use the new words to complete these sentences.

I will look at the _____.

I can hang from the high _____.

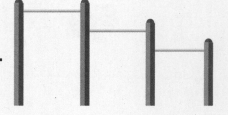

 I will put the bug in a _____.

I don't want to have a _____.

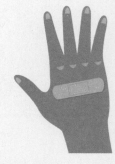

Will It Work?

Fill in the circle to answer **yes** or **no**.

1. You can fix the pants with a needle and thread.

    ○ yes   ○ no

2. You can fix the toy car with a rubber band.

    ○ yes   ○ no

3. You can fix the doorknob with tape.

    ○ yes   ○ no

4. You can fix the flower with glue.

    ○ yes   ○ no

What would you use to fix a cut on your hand?

Reading Color Words

Read the words. Color the buttons.

blue

red

orange

green

purple

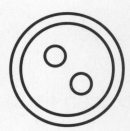

brown

pink

yellow

black

What Do You Hear?

Fill in the circle under the vowel sound you hear.

a   e   i   o   u

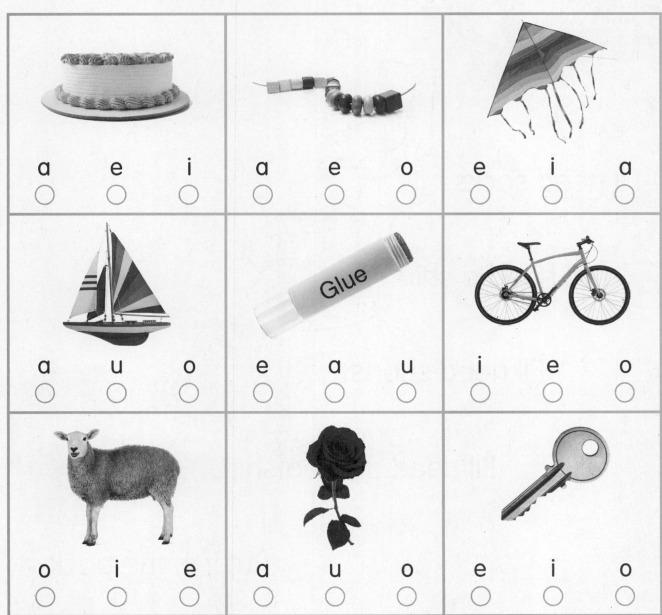

| a | e | i | a | e | o | e | i | a |
| ○ | ○ | ○ | ○ | ○ | ○ | ○ | ○ | ○ |

| a | u | o | e | a | u | i | e | o |
| ○ | ○ | ○ | ○ | ○ | ○ | ○ | ○ | ○ |

| o | i | e | a | u | o | e | i | o |
| ○ | ○ | ○ | ○ | ○ | ○ | ○ | ○ | ○ |

Put It in the Pack

I'm going on a camping trip.
I will put the things
I need in my pack.

I'll need socks.

I'll need a shirt.

I'll need shorts.

I'll need a sweatshirt.

Put it in the pack.

I'll need a hat.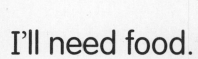

I'll need food.

I'll need my sleeping bag.

I'll need a flashlight.

I'll need Teddy.

Put me in the pack!

I'll put the pack on my back.
Help! I can't move.

I can't hike to the camp.
I'll take out a few things.

I don't have to have socks.

I don't have to have a shirt.

I don't have to have shorts.

I don't have to have a sweatshirt.

I don't have to have a hat.

I don't have to have food.

I don't have to have a sleeping bag.

I don't have to have a flashlight.

Teddy and I are ready!

Let's go!

What Did It Say?

Fill in a circle to answer each question.

1. Where is the little boy going?

○   ○   ○

2. How will the little boy carry his things?

○   ○   ○

3. What is the little boy's problem?

○   ○   ○

4. What does the little boy take out that he will need?

○   ○   ○

  Smart Start • EMC 9849 • © Evan-Moor Corp.

Working with Word Families

ack

b + ack = __ __ __ __

p + ack = __ __ __ __

cr + ack = __ __ __ __ __

qu + ack = __ __ __ __ __

sn + ack = __ __ __ __ __

tr + ack = __ __ __ __ __

s + ack = __ __ __ __

r + ack = __ __ __ __

Read the sentence in each box. Draw what it tells you to do.

Draw a dish with a crack.

Draw a snack you like to eat.

What Would You Do?

Fill in the circle for the correct answer.

What would you do if your pack was too heavy?

⚪ Take something out. ⚪ Put something in.

What would you do if it got dark?

⚪ Turn off the flashlight. ⚪ Turn on the flashlight.

What would you do if you got hungry?

⚪ Eat a snack. ⚪ Go to bed.

What would you do to stay dry in the rain?

⚪ Go outside. ⚪ Go in the tent.

What would you cook on the fire?

⚪ Hot dogs and marshmallows ⚪ Jello and ice cream

Take It Camping!

Circle the things you would take camping.
Draw a line under the ones you would need for school.

Smart Start • EMC 9849 • © Evan-Moor Corp.

Connect the Dots

Start with 1. Draw something you might see on a camping trip.

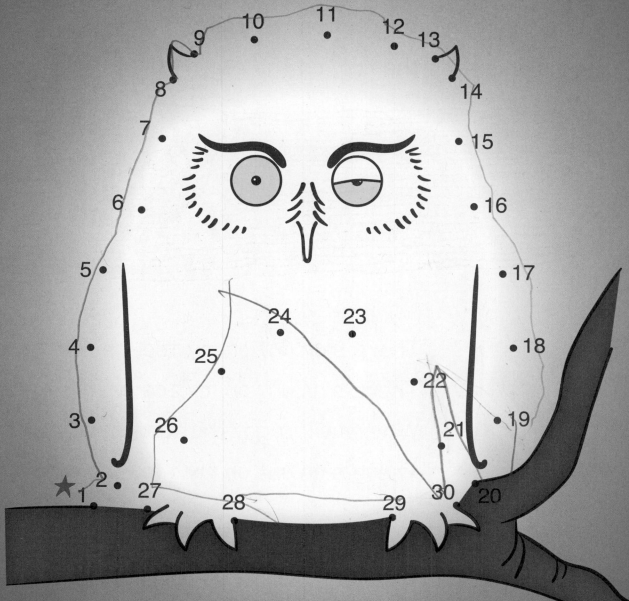

Make a list of animals you might see on a camping trip.

_____   _____   _____

_____   _____   _____

An Ant on the Rug

There's an ant on the rug, on the rug.

There's an ant on the rug, on the rug.

What a tiny bug, little ant on the rug.

There's an ant on the rug, on the rug.

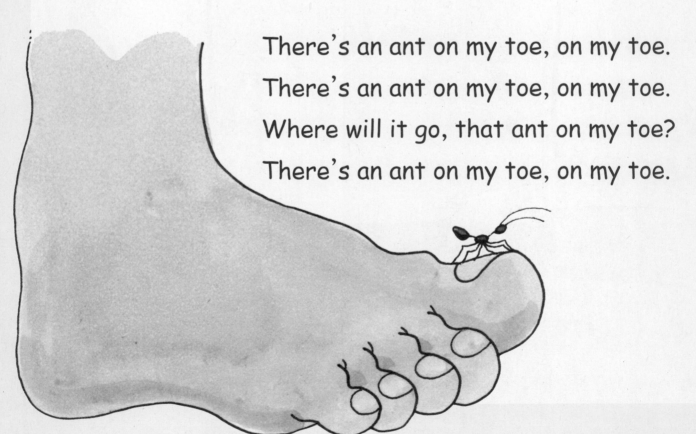

There's an ant on my toe, on my toe.

There's an ant on my toe, on my toe.

Where will it go, that ant on my toe?

There's an ant on my toe, on my toe.

There's an ant on my knee, on my knee.

There's an ant on my knee, on my knee.

It's climbing up on me. Ooooo! An ant on my knee.

There's an ant on my knee, on my knee.

There's an ant on my arm, on my arm.

There's an ant on my arm, on my arm.

It won't do any harm, the ant on my arm.

There's an ant on my arm, on my arm.

There's an ant on my ear, on my ear.

There's an ant on my ear, on my ear.

I have nothing to fear from
the ant on my ear.

There's an ant on my ear, on my ear.

There's an ant on my nose, on my nose.

There's an ant on my nose, on my nose.

What do you suppose? An ant on my nose!

There's an ant on my nose, on my nose.

There's an ant in my hair, in my hair.

There's an ant in my hair, in my hair.

I am very aware there's an ant in my hair.

There's an ant in my hair, in my hair.

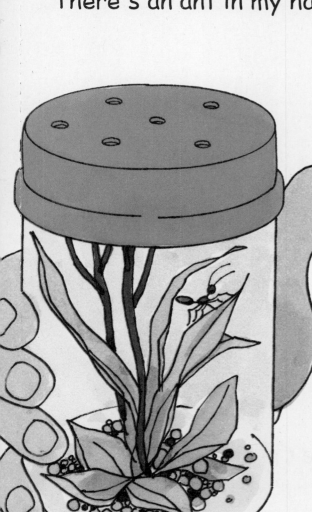

There's an ant in a jar, in a jar.

There's an ant in a jar, in a jar.

It traveled near and far, but
   now it's in a jar.

There's an ant in a jar, in a jar.

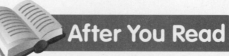

After You Read

Practice your favorite part of
the story. When you can read
it quickly, read it to an adult.

What Did It Say?

Draw a line to show where the ant was.

First

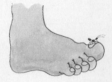

Next

Next

Next

Next

Next

Next

At the end

Do you think the boy was happy to have the ant in the jar?

yes   no

Why do you think the way you do?

_____

_____

Working with Word Families

ug

r + ug = ___ ___ ___   b + ug = ___ ___ ___

d + ug = ___ ___ ___   h + ug = ___ ___ ___

pl + ug = ___ ___ ___ ___   sn + ug = ___ ___ ___ ___

Use the new words to complete these sentences.

Be careful when you touch the _____.

Look at the hole I _____.

Dad gave me a _____.

He's as _____ as

a _____ in a _____.

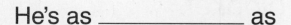

Molly and Max

This is Molly.

This is Max.

They played together all week.

Monday they played hide and seek.

Molly hid under the blanket.

Max hid behind the plant.

Smart Start • EMC 9849 • © Evan-Moor Corp.

Tuesday they dug holes in the yard.

Molly buried a bone.

Max picked some flowers.

Wednesday they went for a walk.

Molly walked and sniffed.

Max walked round and round.

Thursday they learned to open doors.

Molly went in and out.

Max found the trash.

Friday they practiced jumping.

Molly jumped high.

Max jumped too high.

Smart Start • EMC 9849 • © Evan-Moor Corp.

Saturday they chased balls.

Molly brought the balls back.

Max found a bigger ball.

Sunday is a day for rest.

Molly will rest.

Will Max rest, too?

What Did It Say?

Fill in the circles to answer the questions.

1. Which dog hid under the blanket? ○ Max ○ Molly

2. Which dog found the trash? ○ Max ○ Molly

3. Which dog brought the balls back? ○ Max ○ Molly

4. Which dog buried a bone? ○ Max ○ Molly

5. Which dog popped a balloon? ○ Max ○ Molly

6. Which dog picked some flowers? ○ Max ○ Molly

7. Which dog do you think will try
   to open the gifts? ○ Max ○ Molly

8. Which dog is easier to care for? ○ Max ○ Molly

Max Learns the Hard Way

Color, cut, and paste. Put the pictures in order to tell Max's story.

1

paste

2

paste

3

paste

4

paste

59

Trouble!

It's easy for Max to get in trouble. Put a check by the things that would mean **trouble**.

☐ Max chewed the shoe.

☐ Max drank his water.

☐ Max jumped over the gate.

☐ Max chewed on the bone.

☐ Max knocked over the lamp.

☐ Max picked some flowers.

☐ Max took a nap.

☐ Max opened the gifts.

Think about what Max might do next.
Write it here.

_____

Will it mean trouble for Max?   yes   no

Working with Word Families

b + one = ___ ___ ___ ___   c + one = ___ ___ ___ ___

ph + one = ___ ___ ___ ___ ___   st + one = ___ ___ ___ ___ ___

thr + one = ___ ___ ___ ___ ___ ___   z + one = ___ ___ ___ ___

Write the words to label the pictures.

___ ___ ___ ___   ___ ___ ___ ___ ___ ___   ___ ___ ___ ___

___ ___ ___ ___ ___ ___   ___ ___ ___ ___ ___   end ___ ___ ___ ___

What's at the End?

Write the letter that stands for the sound you hear at the end of each word.

do___

doo___

ba___

boo___

cu___

ja___

tu___

bo___

ca___

ma___

Draw a Pup

Follow the steps to draw a puppy.

How is the pup like Max?

_____

How is the pup different from Max?

_____

New Friends

Cookie lived with Amy. She had a dish for water. She had a dish for food. She had a purple mouse with a long tail. She had all that she needed. Cookie loved her home.

One day Amy came home. She had a surprise for Cookie. It was not a new mouse. It was not a new dish. It was a new friend. It was a little gray kitten.

Cookie didn't need a new friend. Cookie ran from Amy. She hid behind the chair.

Smart Start • EMC 9849 • © Evan-Moor Corp.

The new kitten sniffed Cookie's dish. Cookie hissed at the kitten.

The new kitten tasted Cookie's water. Cookie swatted at the kitten.

The new kitten batted Cookie's mouse. Cookie chased the kitten away.

The new kitten cried. It was afraid. Cookie looked at the kitten. It was shaking.

Cookie touched the kitten with her paw. The kitten was soft. Cookie licked the kitten's ear. She licked the kitten's face. The little kitten began to purr.

Cookie didn't need a friend. But the new kitten did. Maybe Cookie could be the new kitten's friend.

Cookie sat on Amy's lap. The little kitten sat next to Cookie. Cookie purred. The little kitten purred.

Cookie played with her mouse. The little kitten played, too.

Cookie curled up for a nap. The little kitten slept. The little kitten had a new friend. Cookie had a new friend, too.

Smart Start • EMC 9849 • © Evan-Moor Corp.

What Did It Say?

Answer each question.
Fill in the circle to mark **yes** or **no**.

1. In the beginning Cookie had

   a dish for water .... ○ yes   ○ no

   a purple bed .... ○ yes   ○ no

   a dish for food .... ○ yes   ○ no

   a yellow mouse .... ○ yes   ○ no

2. Was Cookie happy to see
   Amy's surprise? .... ○ yes   ○ no

3. Cookie

   hissed at the new kitten .... ○ yes   ○ no

   scratched the new kitten .... ○ yes   ○ no

   swatted at the new kitten .... ○ yes   ○ no

   chased the new kitten .... ○ yes   ○ no

4. The new kitten was afraid. .... ○ yes   ○ no

5. Cookie decided to be the new
   kitten's friend. .... ○ yes   ○ no

What Does It Mean?

Look at the pictures. Write the best word in each sentence.

sniffed	tasted	hissed	purred	cried
licked	chased	swatted	played	

The kitten _____ the flower.

Cookie _____ at the kitten.

Cookie _____ the kitten.

The little kitten _____.

The kitten _____ with the yarn.

Cookie _____ the kitten's ear.

 Smart Start • EMC 9849 • © Evan-Moor Corp.

Animal Babies

Cut and paste to match the babies with the parents.
Write the names under the pictures.

chick   calf   piglet   pup   foal   kitten

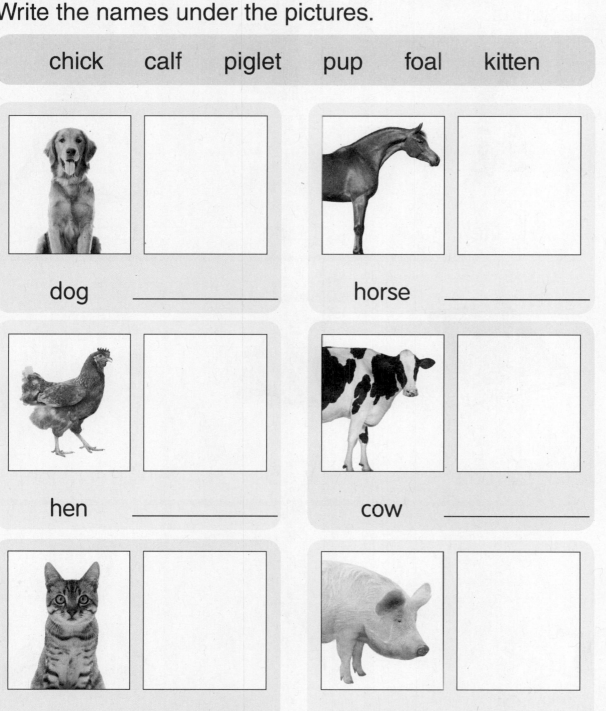

dog _____

horse _____

hen _____

cow _____

cat _____

pig _____

7-25-18

The Sound of k

Say the picture name. Write the letter **k** where you hear its sound.

Kitten   Kite   Kangaroo

Book   Koala   Doorknob

Saw   Key   King

7-25-18

Working with Word Families

ace

f + ace = f A C e   l + ace = l A C ⌀ e

r + ace = r A C e   pl + ace = P l A C e

sp + ace = S P A C e   tr + ace = t r A C e

Finish each picture. The words tell you what to do.

Draw a face.

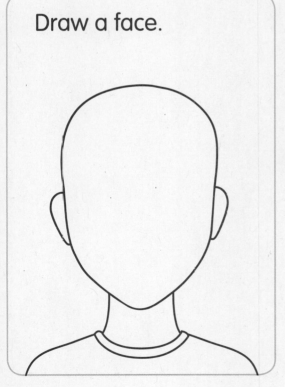

Draw the cars in the race.

What Do You Think?

Fill in the circle in front of **yes** or **no**.

Can two cats be friends?   ○ yes   ○ no

Can two cats drive to the mall?   ○ yes   ○ no

Can two cats like the same toy?   ○ yes   ○ no

Can two cats chase one another?   ○ yes   ○ no

Can two cats lap the milk?   ○ yes   ○ no

Can two cats write a letter?   ○ yes   ○ no

Draw something two cats could really do.

The Missing Mitten

One day Maria got ready to go outside. It was a cold, snowy day. Maria put on her snow pants. She put on her jacket. She put on her purple stocking hat. Her mother gave her a scarf to keep her neck warm. Next she pulled on her shiny purple snow boots. They were new. Maria couldn't wait to try them out. She was almost ready. All that she needed were her mittens.

Maria reached into her jacket pocket. She pulled
out one fuzzy blue mitten. One mitten? Where was the
other mitten? Maria looked all over. She looked like a
marshmallow stumbling around her room. Where was the
missing mitten?

Maria yelled to her mom, "Hey, Mom! I can only find
one blue mitten. Will you help me find the other one?"

Maria's mom came into her room. She took one look at Maria and started to laugh.

Maria frowned. "What are you laughing at?" she asked.

Maria's mom pulled Maria in front of the mirror. She pointed to Maria's purple stocking hat. Peeking out from under the hat was a blue thumb. A hat with a blue thumb?

Maria reached up and pulled off the hat. There was the missing mitten!

What Did It Say?

Fill in the circle or write words to answer the questions.

1. What was missing?

   ○ hat   ○ scarf   ○ mitten

2. Who did the missing thing belong to?

   ○ Mom   ○ Maria   ○ Dad

3. Where was the missing thing found?

   _____

Draw something that belongs to you that was missing.

Put It in Order

Color, cut, and paste. Show the order that Maria put on her things before she went outside.

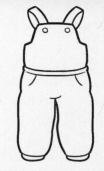

1

paste

2

paste

3

paste

4

paste

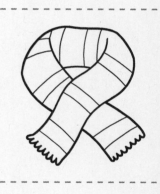

5

paste

6

paste

Whose Mittens?

Read the sentences. Then label the mittens.
Use **'s** after the name of the owner.

Tommy has fuzzy mittens with bears on them.

Molly has stripes on her mittens.

Baby has pink mittens with bows on them.

Dad has big blue mittens with metal clips.

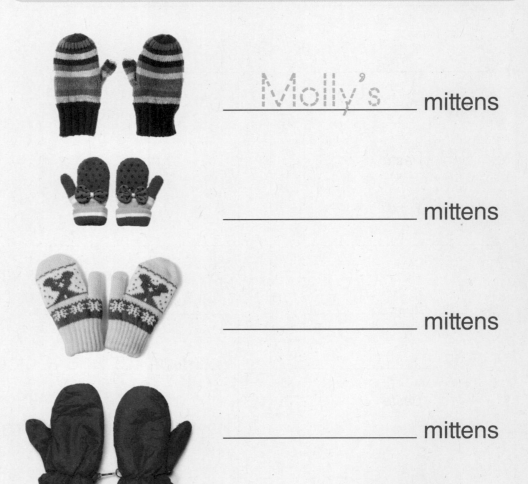

_____Molly's_____ mittens

_____ mittens

_____ mittens

_____ mittens

Working with Word Families
itten

m + itten = __ __ __ __ __ __

k + itten = __ __ __ __ __ __

b + itten = __ __ __ __ __ __

wr + itten = __ __ __ __ __ __ __

Use the new words to complete these sentences.

1. The dog was _____ by a flea.

2. My name is _____ in this book.

3. The _____ has soft fur and a nice meow.

4. The _____ keeps my hand warm when it's cold.

Make Them the Same

Color the second mitten to match the first.
List three words that tell about the mittens.

1. _____

2. _____

3. _____

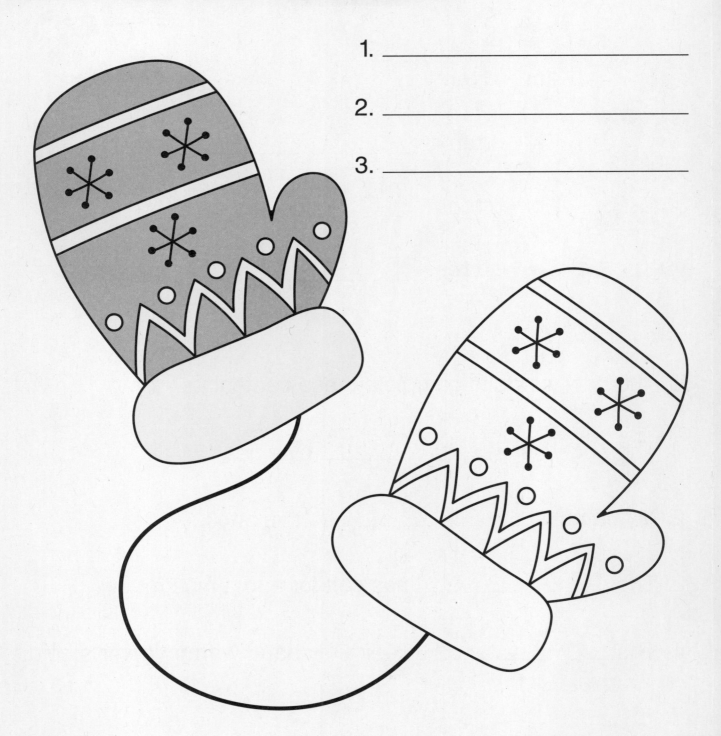

Color Crossword

Use color words to fill in the blanks of this crossword.

black	blue	brown	gray	green	orange
pink	purple	red	white	yellow	

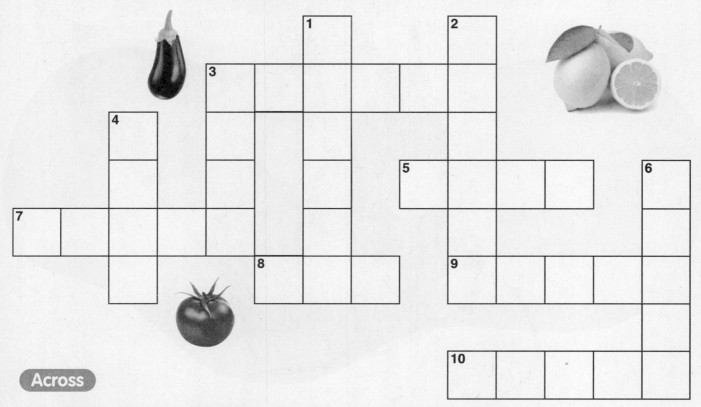

Across

3. What color is grape juice and an eggplant?

5. What color is the sky on a sunny day?

7. What color is soot from a fire?

8. What color are ripe tomatoes?

9. What color is the snow?

10. What color is hot chocolate?

Down

1. What color is a ripe pumpkin?

2. What color is a lemon?

3. What color is a cat's tongue?

4. What color is made from black and white?

6. What color is spinach?

A Mitten

Practice this page until you can read it with no mistakes.
Read it to an adult.

a mitten

a big mitten

a big red mitten

a big red mitten with white dots

a big red mitten with white dots and blue stars

A New Neighbor

Peter looked down from his window. There was a big moving van next door. He watched as the man unloaded the van.

Peter wanted a new friend—a new friend who could play ball, ride bikes, and build things. Peter watched. The man unloaded a bike, a wagon, and a big bear.

Peter smiled. The new family must have a boy.

Just then a car pulled in behind the moving van. It was the new family. Peter watched. The family got out of the car. There was a boy! He had on a red ball cap. Peter cheered. He watched the new family go inside their house.

Smart Start • EMC 9849 • © Evan-Moor Corp.

Peter ran downstairs. He grabbed his ball and mitt. He ran next door. He knocked on the door. A man opened the door. Peter said, "Hi, I'm Peter. I live next door. Can your kid come out and play ball?"

The man smiled and said, "I'm glad to meet you, Peter. Sam was hoping to meet a new ball-playing friend. Sam loves to play ball. Sam can catch any ball you throw.

Peter smiled. He couldn't wait to meet Sam. It would be fun to have a pal next door.

The man called, "Sam, come meet our new neighbor. This is Peter. Peter, this is Samantha. We call her Sam."

Peter gulped. Samantha? That was a girl's name. His new neighbor was a girl! The kid with the red ball cap was a girl? Peter didn't know what to do. He wanted a new friend. He wanted a pal who could play ball. He had thought that pal would be a boy.

Sam smiled at Peter. "Hi, Peter, want to play some catch?"

Peter nodded. He wondered if Sam could really catch. Her dad said she could catch anything.

Smart Start • EMC 9849 • © Evan-Moor Corp.

Later Peter and Sam drank milk and ate cookies. Peter shook his head and smiled. "Sam, your dad was right. You can catch anything I throw. And you throw a mean fast ball, too. I'm glad that you moved next door to me."

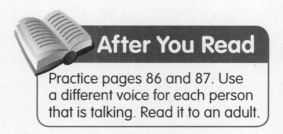

After You Read

Practice pages 86 and 87. Use a different voice for each person that is talking. Read it to an adult.

What Did It Say?

Fill in the circle to show the answer.

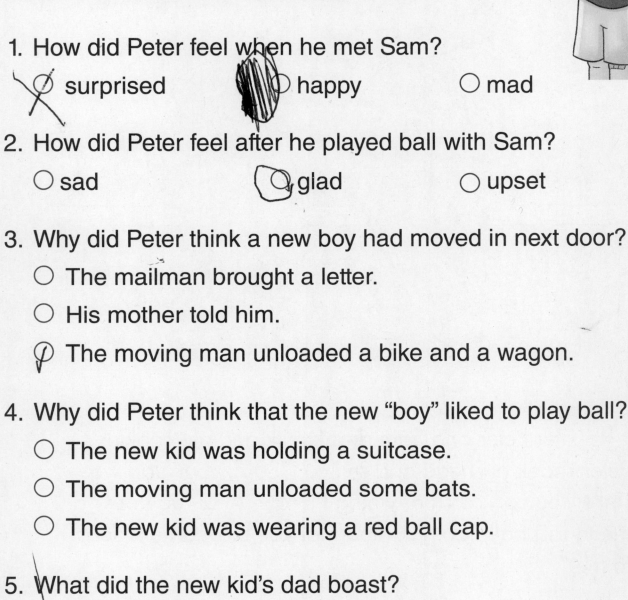

1. How did Peter feel when he met Sam?

   ⊘ surprised   ○ happy   ○ mad

2. How did Peter feel after he played ball with Sam?

   ○ sad   ○ glad   ○ upset

3. Why did Peter think a new boy had moved in next door?

   ○ The mailman brought a letter.

   ○ His mother told him.

   ○ The moving man unloaded a bike and a wagon.

4. Why did Peter think that the new "boy" liked to play ball?

   ○ The new kid was holding a suitcase.

   ○ The moving man unloaded some bats.

   ○ The new kid was wearing a red ball cap.

5. What did the new kid's dad boast?

   ○ He said that Sam was a good hitter.

   ○ He said that Sam was a good pitcher.

   ○ He said that Sam could catch any ball Peter threw.

7-21-18

Baseball Words

Use the words below to label the drawing.

~~baseball~~ ~~mitt~~ ball cap ~~cleats~~
~~homeplate~~ ~~bat~~ ~~backstop~~ ~~batting glove~~

bɔt

ball cap

batting glove

bɑcκ2тɵρ

baseball

Mitt

cleɑtᵹ

ｈoﾝe pɩＵe

The Sound of gr

Circle the pictures whose names begin with the sound that **gr** stands for.

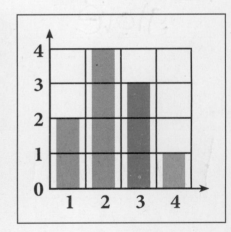

1. What **gr**ade are you in? _____

2. Is the **gr**ass **gr**een? _____

3. Are you ever **gr**umpy? _____

Smart Start • EMC 9849 • © Evan-Moor Corp.

Draw a Story

Cut and paste the sentences in order. Then draw the story.

1

paste

2

paste

3

paste

4

paste

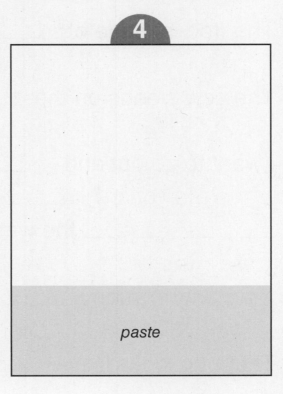

The ball was thrown.

Billy hit the ball hard.

Billy came to the plate.

It was a home run.

Working with Word Families
ay

d + ay = ___ ___ ___   pl + ay = ___ ___ ___ ___

cl + ay = ___ ___ ___ ___   str + ay = ___ ___ ___ ___ ___

h + ay = ___ ___ ___   spr + ay = ___ ___ ___ ___ ___

Use the new words to complete these sentences.

1. The frog is made of _____.

2. The cow sleeps on the _____.

3. I want to go out and _____.

4. _____ the water on the flowers.

5. It's a bright, sunny _____.

6. That pup looks like a _____.

Smart Start • EMC 9849 • © Evan-Moor Corp.

Reading

_____
Name

I read stories and practiced phonics skills. Now I'm an even better reader!

I did activities that helped me improve my reading comprehension skills.

_____
Date

You Completed the Section
GOOD WORK!

Smart Start • EMC 9849 • © Evan-Moor Corp.

Math Skills

Helping Your Child Learn Math Skills

Children use math at home and at school. They identify numbers, count, and use other math skills to solve real-life problems. The activities in this section provide practice with addition, subtraction, fractions, telling time, and many other math skills that your child needs to be successful in school and well-prepared for life.

Addition, Subtraction, and Basic Math Skills

A variety of math activities help your child practice addition and subtraction, comparing values, graphing, patterning, place value, and and many more basic math skills. The engaging tasks provide rigorous practice that prepares your child to work with larger numbers.

Word Problems

Addition and subtraction word problems provide practice with real-life math problems and critical thinking skills. Encourage your child to discuss the word problems and talk about the operations that can be used to solve them.

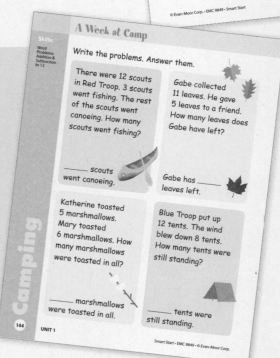

Measurement, Money, and Time

Activities that practice nonstandard measurement, counting the values of coins, and telling time provide practice with math skills your child can use every day.

Test Your Skills

Each themed section ends with a Test Your Skills activity page that provides your child with focused tasks for the math skills they have just practiced. These tests serve as an indicator of your child's understanding of the math skills.

Certificate

After your child completes the math section of this book, remove the math certificate and have your child write his or her name on it. Congratulate your child on a job well done and post the certificate in a prominent place.

Count and Tell

Skills:

Counting 0–10

Note: You may need to help your child read the word problems.

How many legs?

 has _____ legs.

How many ears?

has _____ ears.

How many feet in all?

_____ feet in all.

How many balls?

has _____ balls.

What is the largest answer? _____

What is the smallest answer? _____

Gone to the Dogs

98

Note: You may need to help your child read the word problems.

Skills:

One-to-One
Correspondence

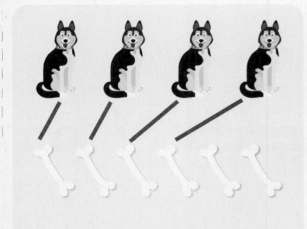

_____ bones

were used.

_____ doghouses

were used.

_____ bowls of food

were used.

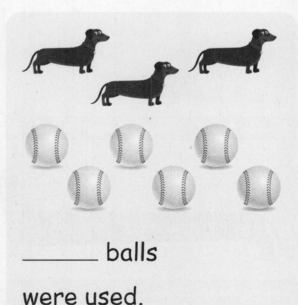

_____ balls

were used.

What is the largest number of things used? _____

What is the smallest number of things used? _____

Gone to the Dogs

How long is each thing?

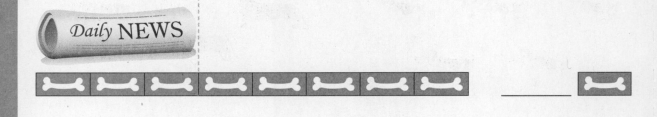

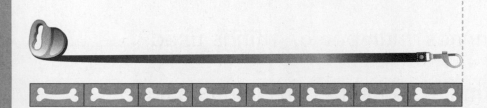

Smart Start • EMC 9849 • © Evan-Moor Corp.

Gone to the Dogs

Skills:

Reading Graphs

Read the graph. Answer the questions.

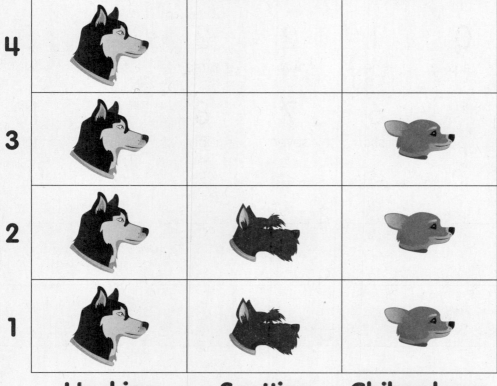

	Huskies	Scotties	Chihuahuas

1. How many dogs are in the store?

    _____   _____   _____

2. How many dogs in all? _____

3. Are there more 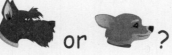 or ?

4. Which dog is there the most of?

Gone to the Dogs

Number Words

Write each number word.

0	**1**	**2**	**3**	**4**	**5**
zero	one	two	three	four	five
6	**7**	**8**	**9**	**10**	
six	seven	eight	nine	ten	

3 _____   2 _____   1 _____

10 _____   9 _____   6 _____

0 _____   4 _____   5 _____

7 _____   8 _____

Count and match.

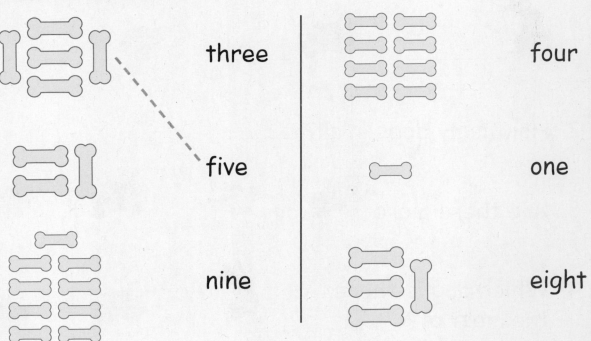

three

five

nine

four

one

eight

Smart Start • EMC 9849 • © Evan-Moor Corp.

Gone to the Dogs

Skills:

More, Less

Larger, Smaller

Write the numbers. Circle the set with more.

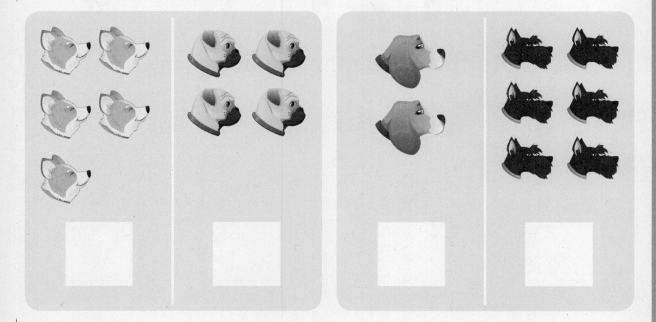

Write the numbers. Circle the set with less.

Which number is larger?   5 or 8   3 or 1

Which number is smaller?   7 or 2   9 or 0

Gone to the Dogs

Note: Use this assessment after your child has completed pages 98–103.

Count the dots. Write the number to tell how many.

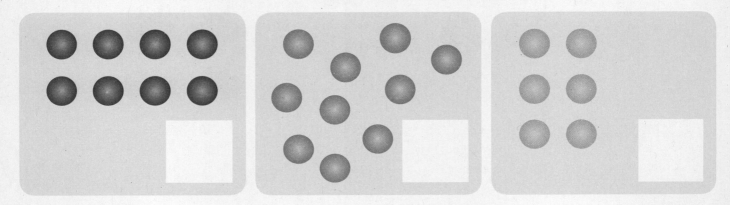

Fill in the circle to show how long it is.

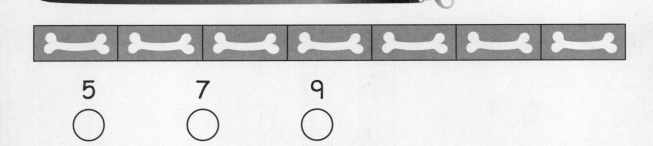

5   7   9
○   ○   ○

Color the shapes.

Skills:
Addition to 6

Add.

$1 + 2 = \underline{}$

$1 + 4 = \underline{}$

$3 + 1 = \underline{}$

$6 + 0 = \underline{}$

Write and add.

$\underline{1} + \underline{1} = \underline{2}$

$\underline{} + \underline{} = \underline{}$

$\underline{} + \underline{} = \underline{}$

$\underline{} + \underline{} = \underline{}$

On the Farm

Add. Color.

1 = black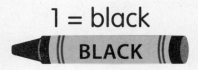
BLACK

3 = yellow
YELLOW

5 = brown
BROWN

2 = pink
PINK

4 = green
GREEN

6 = blue
BLUE

5 + 1

0 + 1

1 + 2

3 + 1

1 + 1

2 + 2

2 + 3

Add.

2 + 4 = _____   3 + 2 = _____   4 + 0 = _____

3 + 3 = _____   1 + 5 = _____   4 + 1 = _____

On the Farm

Note: You may need to help your child read the word problems.

Add.

2 chickens.
2 more chickens come.
How many chickens?

____ + ____ = ____

____ chickens

3 roosters.
3 more roosters come.
How many roosters?

____ + ____ = ____

____ roosters

0 goats.
5 goats come.
How many goats?

____ + ____ = ____

____ goats

2 sheep.
1 more sheep comes.
How many sheep?

____ + ____ = ____

____ sheep

on the Farm

Skills:

Addition to 6

Add.

2 + 2 = _____   3 + 2 = _____   4 + 2 = _____

1 + 2 = _____   0 + 2 = _____   1 + 1 = _____

3 + 1 = _____   1 + 0 = _____   0 + 3 = _____

0 + 0 = _____   2 + 3 = _____   3 + 3 = _____

3	2	0	3	0
+ 1	+ 3	+ 3	+ 3	+ 0

1	4	4	2	1
+ 0	+ 2	+ 1	+ 2	+ 1

On the Farm

Smart Start • EMC 9849 • © Evan-Moor Corp.

Count the Pennies

Skills:

Money—Pennies

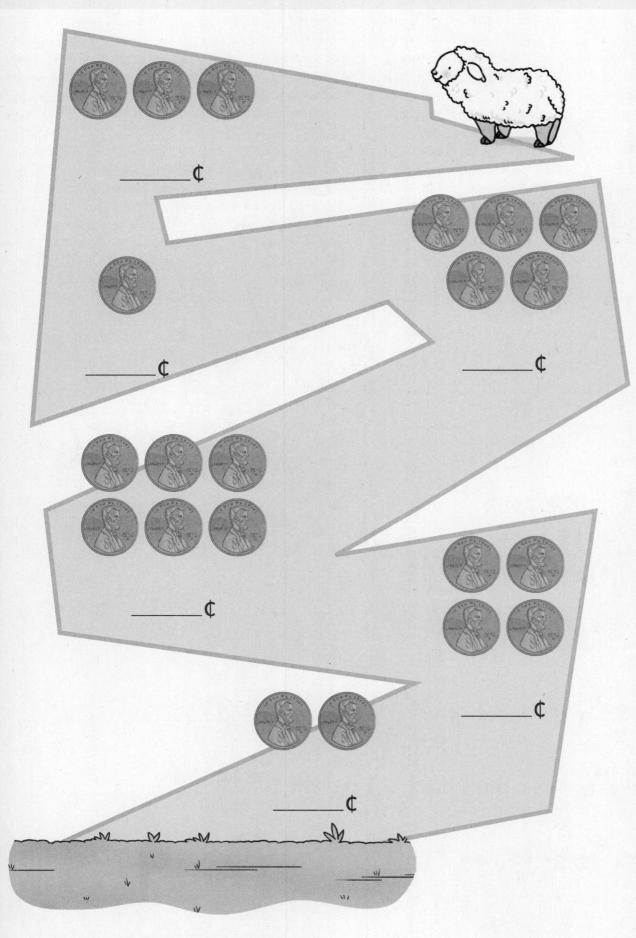

_____ ¢

_____ ¢

_____ ¢

_____ ¢

_____ ¢

_____ ¢

On the Farm

Pigs and Sheep

Tell how many.

1.  in the ◯ ? _____

2.  in the ▢ ? _____

3.  in **both** the ◯ and the ▢ ? _____

4.  in **both** the ◯ and the ▢ ? _____

5.  in the ▢ but **not** in the ◯ ? _____

On the Farm

Skills:

Ordinal Numbers

 first 1st second 2nd third 3rd fourth 4th fifth 5th  sixth 6th

1. Which place is the in? _____

2. Which place is the in? _____

3. Which place is the in? _____

4. Which animal is between the 4th and 6th place?

5. Which animal is between the 2nd and 4th place?

6. Mark the 3rd hen.

7. Mark the 5th dog.

On the Farm

Are Both Sides the Same?

Note: You may need to read the sentence at the bottom of the page to your child.

Circle **yes** or **no**.

yes   no

yes   no

yes   no

yes   no

yes   no

yes   no

yes   no

yes   no

yes   no

On the Farm

When an object is **symmetrical**, both sides
are the same in shape and size.

Note: Use this assessment after your child has completed pages 105–112. Help your child read the directions.

TEST YOUR SKILLS

Count.

Add.   3 + 3 = _____   4 + 2 = _____   1 + 2 = _____

1 + 0 = _____   3 + 2 = _____   4 + 1 = _____

Read the graph. Answer the questions.

1. How many are there? _____

2. How many are there? _____

3. Which two have the same number?

Read and answer.

3 are in the mud. 2 more come.

How many 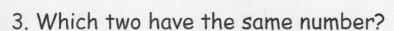 are in the mud?   _____

How Many Bears?

Subtract.

3 – 2 = ___1___

5 – 3 = _____

4 – 0 = _____

6 – 4 = _____

Write and subtract.

___5___ – ___1___ = ___4___

_____ – _____ = _____

_____ – _____ = _____

_____ – _____ = _____

Bears Everywhere

The number of bears is **greater than** the number of fish.

3 ◯ 2

The number of bears is **less than** the number of fish.

2 ◯ 3

Write > or <.

1 ◯ 5

7 ◯ 6

8 ◯ 4

2 ◯ 4

6 ◯ 7

4 ◯ 5

Bears Everywhere

How Many Bears Are Left?

Subtract.

5 – 5 = _____   2 – 1 = _____   6 – 5 = _____

3 – 1 = _____   0 – 0 = _____   4 – 3 = _____

6 – 6 = _____   5 – 2 = _____   3 – 0 = _____

5 – 0 = _____   6 – 2 = _____   1 – 1 = _____

$$\begin{array}{cccc}
5 & 2 & 4 & 5 & 1 \\
-\ 0 & -\ 1 & -\ 3 & -\ 5 & -\ 0 \\
\hline
\end{array}$$

$$\begin{array}{cccc}
6 & 5 & 3 & 5 & 3 \\
-\ 3 & -\ 2 & -\ 0 & -\ 4 & -\ 1 \\
\hline
\end{array}$$

Bears Everywhere

116

Note: Explain to your child that some of these things are much larger in real life.

Measure. Write the number.

The bee is _____ inch long.

The hive is _____ inches.

The fish is _____ inches long.

The berry is _____ inch.

The bear is _____ inches long.

Skills:

Subtraction
to 6

Number Words

Subtract.

$6 - 0 = $ _____ $4 - 2 = $ _____ $3 - 3 = $ _____

$5 - 1 = $ _____ $6 - 3 = $ _____ $5 - 4 = $ _____

$6 - 1 = $ _____ $4 - 3 = $ _____ $3 - 2 = $ _____

$5 - 3 = $ _____ $4 - 0 = $ _____ $6 - 6 = $ _____

Write a word answer.

zero	one	two	three	four	five	six
0	1	2	3	4	5	6

$5 - 5 = $ _____ $3 - 2 = $ _____

$6 - 0 = $ _____ $6 - 2 = $ _____

$4 - 2 = $ _____ $4 - 1 = $ _____

Bears Everywhere

Skills:

Reading
Graphs

Read the graph.

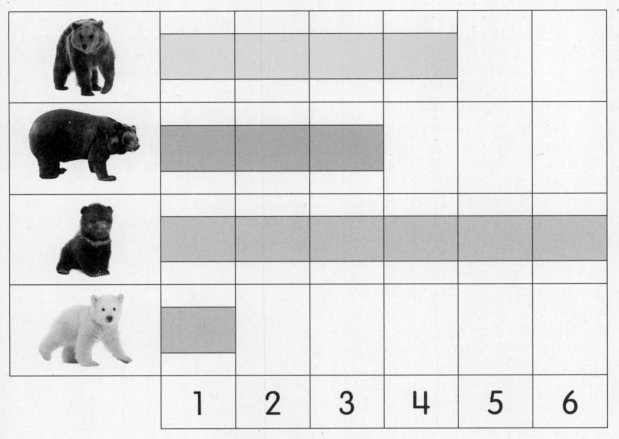

| | 1 | 2 | 3 | 4 | 5 | 6 |

1. How many ? _____

2. How many ? _____

3. How many more than ? _____

4. How many more than ? _____

5. How many more than ? _____

Bears Everywhere

Tally Marks

Tally marks can tell how many.

1	2	3	4	5
|	||	|||	||||	☐

6	7	8	9	10

Use tally marks to make each number.

show 3	show 10	show 5
show 1	show 7	show 2
show 8	show 4	show 6

Count. Write the number.

\|\|\| _____   ☐☐ _____   \| _____

☐ _____   ☐\|\|\|\| _____   ☐\|\|\| _____

Smart Start • EMC 9849 • © Evan-Moor Corp.

TEST YOUR SKILLS

Count. Write the number.

|||| |||| || |||| ||||

_____   _____   _____

Fill in the circle for the answer.

	0	1	2
5 – 5 =	◯	◯	◯
2 – 0 =	◯	◯	◯
4 – 2 =	◯	◯	◯
3 – 1 =	◯	◯	◯

Count the sides and corners.

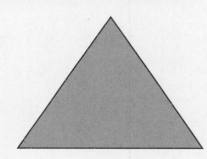

_____ sides

_____ corners

Add.

$$\begin{array}{r} 4 \\ + 3 \\ \hline \end{array}$$

$$\begin{array}{r} 2 \\ + 4 \\ \hline \end{array}$$

$$\begin{array}{r} 8 \\ + 0 \\ \hline \end{array}$$

$$\begin{array}{r} 1 \\ + 5 \\ \hline \end{array}$$

Subtract.

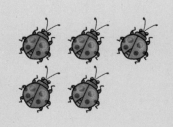

$$\begin{array}{r} 4 \\ - 4 \\ \hline \end{array}$$

$$\begin{array}{r} 6 \\ - 2 \\ \hline \end{array}$$

$$\begin{array}{r} 5 \\ - 3 \\ \hline \end{array}$$

$$\begin{array}{r} 7 \\ - 5 \\ \hline \end{array}$$

Skills:

Patterns

Circle the shape that comes next in each pattern.
Label the patterns.

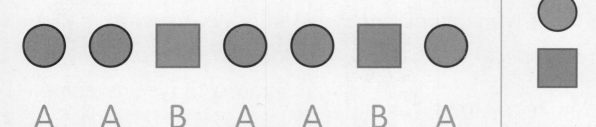

A   A   B   A   A   B   A   _____

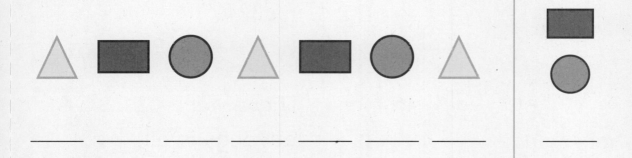

_____   _____   _____   _____   _____   _____   _____   _____

_____   _____   _____   _____   _____   _____   _____   _____

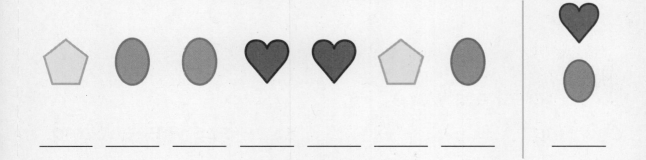

_____   _____   _____   _____   _____   _____   _____   _____

Creepy Crawlies

Bug Problems

Note: You may need to help your child read the word problems.

Write the problems. Answer them.

8 ants were marching.
3 stopped.

How many ants
were still
marching?

_____ ants were still
marching.

4 ladybugs were
looking for aphids.
3 more ladybugs came.

How many
ladybugs
in all?

There were _____
ladybugs in all.

6 crickets were
chirping.
2 more came.

How many crickets
were chirping?

_____ crickets were
chirping.

5 bees were buzzing.
4 stopped.

How many bees
were buzzing?

_____ bee was buzzing.

Creepy Crawlies

Skills:

Telling Time to the Hour

Note: You may need to read the information to your child.

There are 2 hands on a clock.

- The shorter hand is the **hour hand**.
  It points to the hour.

- The longer hand is the **minute hand**.
  It points to 12 when the time is "on the hour."

Write the time.

____ : ____

____ : ____

____ : ____

____ : ____

____ : ____

____ : ____

____ : ____

____ : ____

____ : ____

Creepy Crawlies

Skills:

Addition & Subtraction to 8

Fill in the numbers.

$2 + 3 = \underline{\hspace{1cm}}$

$7 + \underline{\hspace{1cm}} = 7$

$4 + \underline{\hspace{1cm}} = 8$

$8 - \underline{\hspace{1cm}} = 0$

$4 - \underline{\hspace{1cm}} = 1$

$1 + \underline{\hspace{1cm}} = 7$

$4 + 3 = \underline{\hspace{1cm}}$

$7 - 6 = \underline{\hspace{1cm}}$

$6 - \underline{\hspace{1cm}} = 4$

Creepy Crawlies

Smart Start • EMC 9849 • © Evan-Moor Corp.

Skills:

Fractions

How many parts?

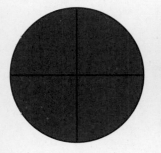
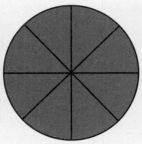
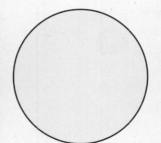
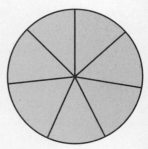

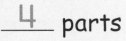 __4__ parts   _____ parts   _____ part   _____ parts

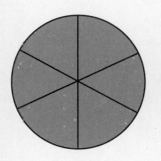
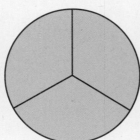
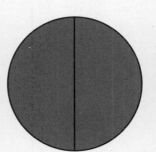
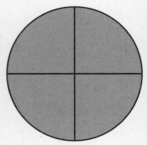

_____ parts   _____ parts   _____ parts   _____ parts

Which ones have 2 equal parts? Circle them.

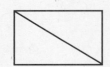

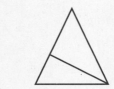

Which ones have 3 equal parts? Circle them.

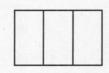

Creepy Crawlies

Ladybugs Are Everywhere!

Add or subtract. Color the ladybugs that = 6.

$0 + 1$

$5 + 1$

$0 + 5$

$6 - 1$

$4 - 1$

$3 - 3$

$7 + 1$

$2 + 4$

$7 - 4$

$9 - 3$

$7 - 2$

Add or subtract. Color the ladybugs that = 3.

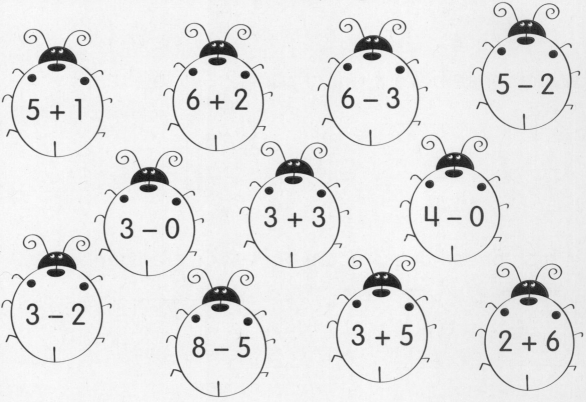

$5 + 1$

$6 + 2$

$6 - 3$

$5 - 2$

$3 - 0$

$3 + 3$

$4 - 0$

$3 - 2$

$8 - 5$

$3 + 5$

$2 + 6$

Creepy Crawlies

128

Write the problems. Answer them.

6 snails were crawling.
3 stopped to
take a nap.

How many
snails were
still crawling?

_____ snails were still
crawling.

1 dragonfly was flying.
3 more dragonflies
came.

How many
dragonflies
were flying?

_____ dragonflies were
flying.

6 grasshoppers
were eating grass.
All 6 hopped away.

How many
grasshoppers
were still
eating grass?

_____ grasshoppers
were still eating grass.

2 butterflies were
sipping nectar. 4 more
butterflies came.

How many
butterflies
were sipping
nectar?

_____ butterflies were
sipping nectar.

Creepy Crawlies

TEST YOUR SKILLS

Add or subtract.

3 + 5 = _____   6 + 2 = _____   8 – 1 = _____   7 – 4 = _____

8 – 5 = _____   8 + 0 = _____   3 + 2 = _____   7 – 7 = _____

Measure.

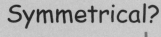

The caterpillar is

_____ inches long.

Write the time.

_____ : _____   _____ : _____

Symmetrical?

yes   no   yes   no

> or <?

7 ◯ 4   2 ◯ 8

What is colored?

$\frac{1}{4}$ $\frac{1}{2}$ $\frac{1}{3}$

Finish the pattern. Label it.

_____ _____ _____ _____ _____ _____ _____ _____ _____ _____

Skills:

Addition to 10

A number line can help you add.

$$4 + 5 = ?$$

Put a ✏ on 4.

Count forward 5 spaces. The answer is 9.

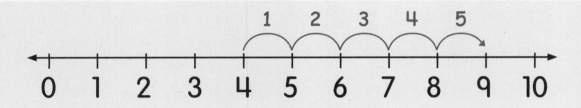

0 1 2 3 4 5 6 7 8 9 10

6 + 4 = _____

4 + 4 = _____   2 + 7 = _____

5 + 4 = _____   5 + 5 = _____

3 + 7 = _____

8 + 2 = _____

6 + 3 = _____

At the Zoo

Counting Back

A number line can help you subtract.

$$9 - 3 = ?$$

Put a ✏ on 9.

Count back 3 spaces. The answer is 6.

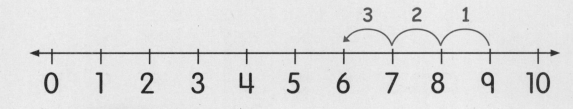

9 − 9 = _____   10 − 2 = _____

9 − 5 = _____   10 − 8 = _____

9 − 6 = _____   10 − 9 = _____

9 − 2 = _____   10 − 4 = _____

Write the answers in order from smallest to greatest.

_____, _____, _____, _____, _____, _____, _____, _____

Smart Start • EMC 9849 • © Evan-Moor Corp.

Skills:

Counting by 10s

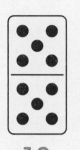    

10   20   _____   _____   _____

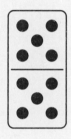  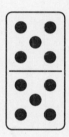  

_____   _____   _____   _____   _____

Connect the dots. Start at 10.

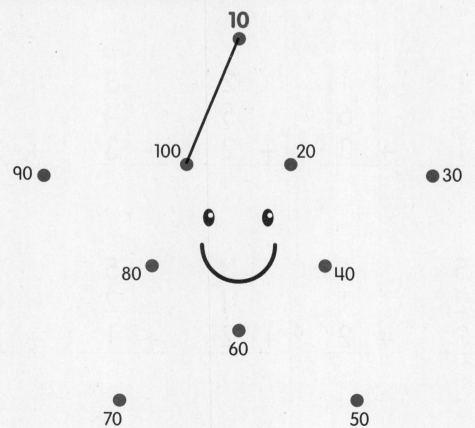

At the Zoo

Add Three Numbers

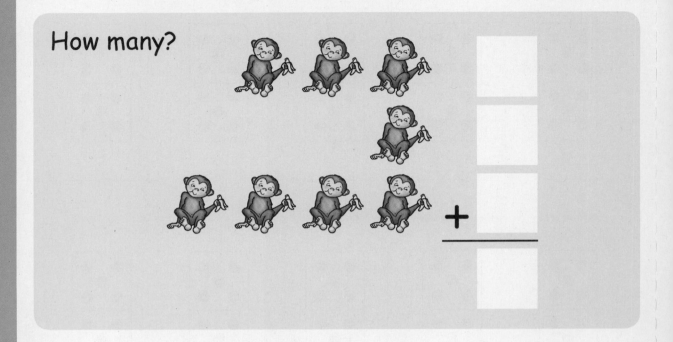

How many?

```
  2        3        6        4        8
  3        5        1        3        0
+ 4      + 1      + 2      + 1      + 2
____     ____     ____     ____     ____
```

```
  1        1        2        3        4
  7        6        5        4        3
+ 1      + 3      + 2      + 3      + 2
____     ____     ____     ____     ____
```

```
  5        6        3        5        7
  2        1        4        2        0
+ 3      + 2      + 2      + 1      + 2
____     ____     ____     ____     ____
```

Skills:

Place Value—
Tens & Ones

Circle groups of 10 animals. How many tens did you make? How many were left?

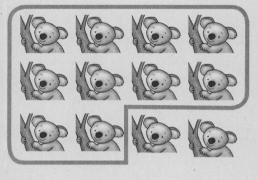

_____ ten + _____ ones = _____

_____ ten + _____ ones = _____

_____ ten + _____ ones = _____

_____ ten + _____ ones = _____

_____ ten + _____ ones = _____

_____ tens + _____ ones = _____

At the Zoo

Mystery Boxes

Write the missing numbers.

Make 7

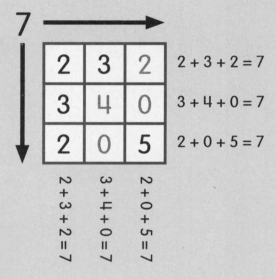

7 →

2	3	2	2 + 3 + 2 = 7
3	4	0	3 + 4 + 0 = 7
2	0	5	2 + 0 + 5 = 7

2 + 3 + 2 = 7   3 + 4 + 0 = 7   2 + 0 + 5 = 7

Make 8

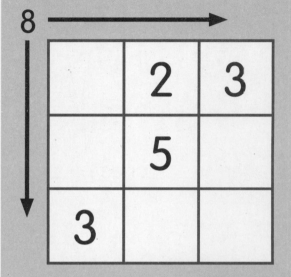

8 →

	2	3
	5	
3		

Make 9

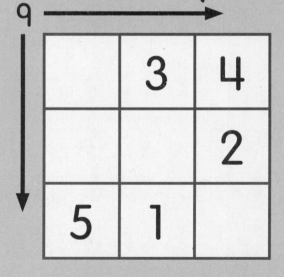

9 →

	3	4
		2
5	1	

Make 10

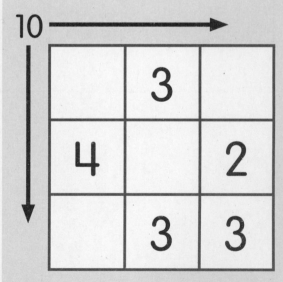

10 →

	3	
4		2
	3	3

Smart Start • EMC 9849 • © Evan-Moor Corp.

Match.

5¢

1¢

nickel

penny

 8¢

 12¢

 10¢

 15¢

At the Zoo

TEST YOUR SKILLS

How many?

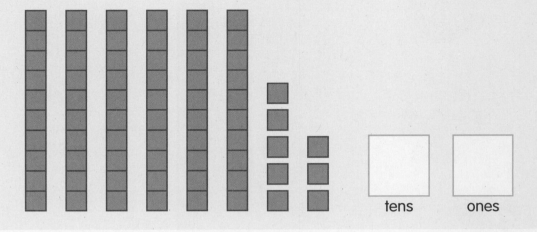

tens   ones

Add or subtract.

6 + 4 = _____   10 – 0 = _____

8 + 2 = _____   9 – 4 = _____

Fill in the circle to show how much.

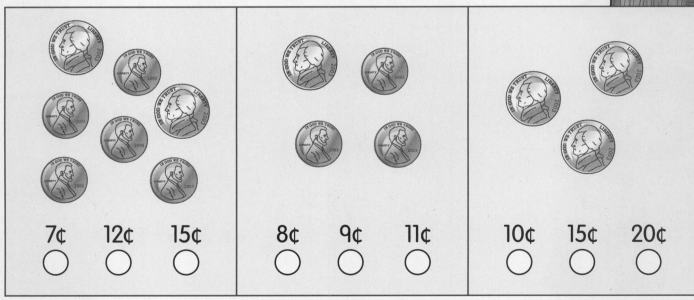

7¢   12¢   15¢   8¢   9¢   11¢   10¢   15¢   20¢
○   ○   ○   ○   ○   ○   ○   ○   ○

Skills:

Addition &
Subtraction
to 12

Match each problem to its answer.

6 + 5

10 − 0

4 + 8

12 − 3

9 + 3

12 − 4

9 + 2

11 − 2

8 + 3

12 − 5

4 + 4

11 − 4

Camping

Number Families

Number families have 2 addition problems and 2 subtraction problems made from 3 numbers.

3 numbers: **7, 5, 12**

2 addition problems	2 subtraction problems
$7 + 5 = 12$	$12 - 7 = 5$
$5 + 7 = 12$	$12 - 5 = 7$

Complete each number family.

8, 3, 11

____ + ____ = ____

____ + ____ = ____

____ − ____ = ____

____ − ____ = ____

9, 2, 11

____ + ____ = ____

____ + ____ = ____

____ − ____ = ____

____ − ____ = ____

8, 4, 12

____ + ____ = ____

____ + ____ = ____

____ − ____ = ____

____ − ____ = ____

9, 3, 12

____ + ____ = ____

____ + ____ = ____

____ − ____ = ____

____ − ____ = ____

camping

Skills:

Addition to 12

How to:

1. Put the larger number in your head.
2. Count on. Write each number on a boot.

9 + 3 = ?
Put 9 in your head.
Add the 3 by counting on.

9 + 3 = __12__

8 + 4 = _____

7 + 4 = _____

7 + 5 = _____

6 + 6 = _____

Camping

Use the sleeping bags to help you find the answers.

$11 - 9 =$ _____ $11 - 5 =$ _____

$11 - 7 =$ _____ $11 - 4 =$ _____

$12 - 4 =$ _____ $12 - 6 =$ _____

$12 - 9 =$ _____ $12 - 3 =$ _____

Camping

Skills:

Reading
Graphs

Read the graph. Answer the questions.

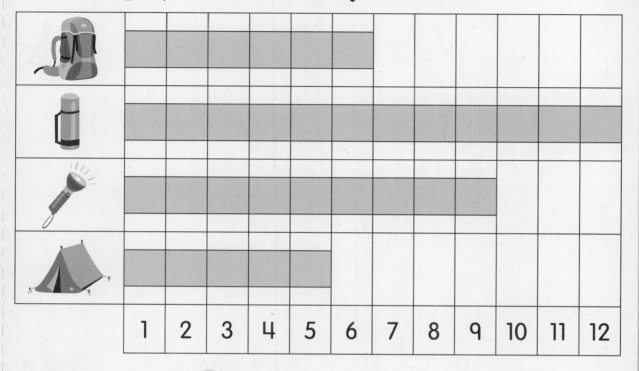

| | 1 | 2 | 3 | 4 | 5 | 6 | 7 | 8 | 9 | 10 | 11 | 12 |

1. How many 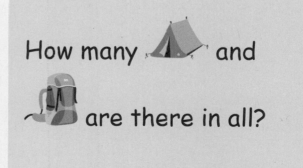 are there? _____

2. How many are there? _____

3. Are there more or more ?

Write the problems. Answer them.

How many more
than are there?

_____

How many and
are there in all?

_____

Camping

A Week at Camp

Write the problems. Answer them.

There were 12 scouts in Red Troop. 3 scouts went fishing. The rest of the scouts went canoeing. How many scouts went canoeing?

_____ scouts went canoeing.

Gabe collected 11 leaves. He gave 5 leaves to a friend. How many leaves does Gabe have left?

Gabe has _____ leaves left.

Katherine toasted 5 marshmallows. Mary toasted 6 marshmallows. How many marshmallows were toasted in all?

_____ marshmallows were toasted in all.

Blue Troop put up 12 tents. The wind blew down 8 tents. How many tents were still standing?

_____ tents were still standing.

Camping

Skills:

Addition & Subtraction to 12

Write the letter that goes with each number.

A $\begin{array}{r} 12 \\ -\ 7 \\ \hline \end{array}$ **F** $\begin{array}{r} 12 \\ -11 \\ \hline \end{array}$ **K** $\begin{array}{r} 8 \\ +3 \\ \hline \end{array}$ **M** $\begin{array}{r} 2 \\ +1 \\ \hline \end{array}$

N $\begin{array}{r} 10 \\ -\ 6 \\ \hline \end{array}$ **O** $\begin{array}{r} 7 \\ -7 \\ \hline \end{array}$ **R** $\begin{array}{r} 3 \\ +9 \\ \hline \end{array}$ **S** $\begin{array}{r} 7 \\ +1 \\ \hline \end{array}$

T $\begin{array}{r} 12 \\ -\ 2 \\ \hline \end{array}$ **U** $\begin{array}{r} 11 \\ -\ 9 \\ \hline \end{array}$ **W** $\begin{array}{r} 0 \\ +6 \\ \hline \end{array}$ **Y** $\begin{array}{r} 11 \\ -\ 4 \\ \hline \end{array}$

$\frac{\quad}{8}\ \frac{\quad}{10}\ \frac{A}{5}\ \frac{\quad}{7} \qquad \frac{A}{5}\ \frac{\quad}{6}\ \frac{A}{5}\ \frac{\quad}{7}$

$\frac{\quad}{1}\ \frac{\quad}{12}\ \frac{\quad}{0}\ \frac{\quad}{3}$

$\frac{\quad}{8}\ \frac{\quad}{11}\ \frac{\quad}{2}\ \frac{\quad}{4}\ \frac{\quad}{11}\ \frac{\quad}{8}\ !$

Camping

Lots of Sticks

How many tens and ones in these numbers?

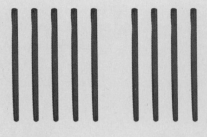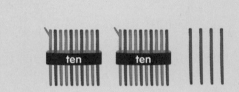

___**2**___ tens and ___**9**___ ones = **29**

_____ tens and _____ ones = **26**

_____ tens and _____ ones = **24**

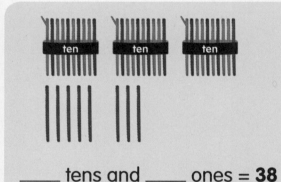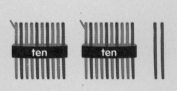

_____ tens and _____ ones = **38**

_____ tens and _____ ones = **22**

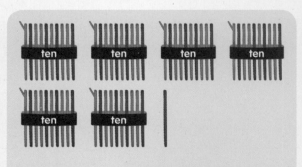

_____ tens and _____ ones = **49**

_____ tens and _____ ones = **61**

Smart Start • EMC 9849 • © Evan-Moor Corp.

Add or subtract.

12 − 8 = _____   11 − 0 = _____   9 + 3 = _____   7 + 5 = _____

12 − 4 = _____   8 + 4 = _____   6 − 4 = _____   7 + 7 = _____

Would you use a 🥄 or a 🥤 to fill the bucket?

spoon   cup

Does a ladybug weigh more than you or less than you?

more   less

Does a hippo weigh more than you or less than you?

more   less

Count by 1s.

75 _____ _____

_____ _____ _____

_____ _____ 83

Write the problem and answer it.

Jason had 12 trading cards. He gave 7 to his sister. How many trading cards does Jason have left?

Jason has _____ trading cards left.

Count by 10s to 100.

_____, _____, _____, _____, _____, _____, _____, _____, _____, _____

How many tens and ones?

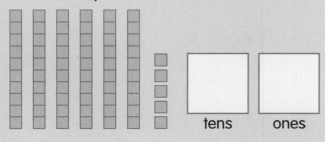

tens   ones

Add or subtract.

$$\begin{array}{r} 22 \\ + 45 \end{array} \qquad \begin{array}{r} 36 \\ - 14 \end{array} \qquad \begin{array}{r} 57 \\ - 33 \end{array} \qquad \begin{array}{r} 61 \\ + 28 \end{array}$$

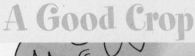

Add or subtract.
Circle the answers that are
the same as 3 + 3 + 3.

$$\begin{array}{r} 14 \\ -\ 7 \\ \hline \end{array} \qquad \begin{array}{r} 6 \\ +\ 8 \\ \hline \end{array} \qquad \begin{array}{r} 14 \\ -\ 9 \\ \hline \end{array} \qquad \begin{array}{r} 7 \\ +\ 7 \\ \hline \end{array}$$

$$\begin{array}{r} 13 \\ -\ 4 \\ \hline \end{array} \qquad \begin{array}{r} 9 \\ +\ 4 \\ \hline \end{array} \qquad \begin{array}{r} 13 \\ -\ 5 \\ \hline \end{array} \qquad \begin{array}{r} 9 \\ +\ 5 \\ \hline \end{array} \qquad \begin{array}{r} 7 \\ +\ 6 \\ \hline \end{array}$$

$$\begin{array}{r} 14 \\ -\ 9 \\ \hline \end{array} \qquad \begin{array}{r} 13 \\ -\ 4 \\ \hline \end{array}$$

Fruity Fun

148

```
    6        2        5        1        3
    4        8        2        6        8
 +  3     +  1     +  2     +  5     +  2
_____ _____ _____ _____ _____


    7        4        9        1        3
    0        4        0        5        4
 +  5     +  4     +  4     +  6     +  5
_____ _____ _____ _____ _____
```

Find the Number Words

```
d f o u r t e e n s q f
b s i x e q i i j r u u
n p u x d q k g d w b l
o h z e r o o f i c v d
h e i g h t u x u t p j
w f w f g f i v e o z b
t e n c t w e l v e n l
f o u r c s e v e n g x
n i n e g d d t h r e e
t w o y c b b i x o n e
k l y v t h i r t e e n
e l e v e n n v s k g a
```

zero
one
two
three
four
five
six
seven
eight
nine
ten
eleven
twelve
thirteen
fourteen

Fruity Fun

What's Growing in the Garden?

Skills:

Word Problems: Addition & Subtraction to 14

Read. Find the sentence that isn't needed.
Mark it out. Write the problems. Answer them.

Dana planted 14 watermelon seeds.

9 of the watermelon seeds sprouted.

~~She ate a slice of watermelon.~~

How many watermelon seeds did **not** sprout?

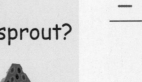

$$\begin{array}{r} 14 \\ -\ 9 \\ \hline 5 \end{array}$$

___5___ seeds did not sprout.

There were 12 grapes in the bunch.

The grapes were delicious!

Gary ate 6 of the grapes.

How many grapes were left?

_____ grapes were left.

Bobby grew 7 plums and 5 strawberries.

The plums were purple.

How many plums and strawberries
did Bobby grow?

Bobby grew _____ plums and strawberries.

Fruity Fun

150

6 + 7 = _____

7 + 6 = _____

13 − 7 = _____

13 − 6 = _____

9 + 4 = _____

4 + 9 = _____

13 − 4 = _____

13 − 9 = _____

8 + 5 = _____

5 + 8 = _____

13 − 8 = _____

13 − 5 = _____

9 + 5 = _____

5 + 9 = _____

14 − 9 = _____

14 − 5 = _____

8 + 4 = _____

4 + 8 = _____

12 − 8 = _____

12 − 4 = _____

8 + 6 = _____

6 + 8 = _____

14 − 6 = _____

14 − 8 = _____

Fruity Fun

Look at the calendar. Answer the questions.

June

Sunday	Monday	Tuesday	Wednesday	Thursday	Friday	Saturday
		1	2	3	4	5
6	7	8	9	10	11	12
13	14	15	16	17	18	19
20	21	22	23	24	25	26
27	28	29	30			

1. What is the name of this month? _____

2. How many days are in this month? _____

3. Flag Day is on what day? _____

4. There is a birthday on _____.

5. There is a soccer game on _____.

6. How many Tuesdays are in this month? _____

7. How many Saturdays are in this month? _____

Smart Start • EMC 9849 • © Evan-Moor Corp.

What's Missing?

after

21 _____

39 _____

45 _____

50 _____

64 _____

77 _____

99 _____

81 _____

before

_____ 47

_____ 50

_____ 36

_____ 64

_____ 21

_____ 92

_____ 63

_____ 33

in between

29 _____ 31

43 _____ 45

38 _____ 40

51 _____ 53

67 _____ 69

80 _____ 82

87 _____ 89

94 _____ 96

Skills:

Counting

Number Order

Fruity Fun

Talking Fruit

Barry Banana has a message for you.
Write the letter that goes with each number.

A
$$14 - 9$$

D
$$8 + 5$$

E
$$13 - 7$$

F
$$7 + 7$$

I
$$9 + 3$$

R
$$11 - 8$$

S
$$13 - 9$$

T
$$13 - 5$$

U
$$14 - 7$$

V
$$14 - 5$$

Y
$$7 + 4$$

___ ___ ___   ___ ___ ___ ___
 6   5   8   14   12   9   6

___ ___ ___ ___ ___ ___
14   3   7   12   8   4

___   ___ ___ ___ !
 5   13   5   11

Skills:

Addition &
Subtraction
to 14

Fruity Fun

154

Smart Start • EMC 9849 • © Evan-Moor Corp.

Farmer Fred likes to keep track of the fruit he sells at his stand. Here is what he sold last Saturday.

8 apples   10 kiwis

5 bananas   7 baskets of raspberries

Color the graph to show what Farmer Fred sold.

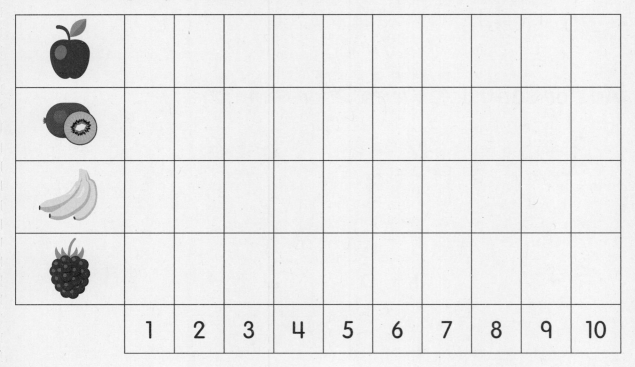

1. How many more kiwis sold than raspberries? _____

2. Which fruit sold the smallest amount? _____

3. How many apples and bananas were sold? _____

Fruity Fun

Greater Than, Less Than

Skills:

Greater Than,
Less Than

(**>**) greater than   (**<**) less than

8 (**>**) 7   7 (**<**) 8

7 ◯ 12   13 ◯ 20   18 ◯ 9

5 ◯ 15   14 ◯ 4   10 ◯ 0

Add or subtract. Write **>** or **<** in the ◯.

9 + 5   12 + 1
☐ ◯ ☐

8 + 5   5 + 6
☐ ◯ ☐

3 + 7   6 + 6
☐ ◯ ☐

5 + 4   8 + 3
☐ ◯ ☐

13 − 8   11 − 4
☐ ◯ ☐

14 − 7   5 + 4
☐ ◯ ☐

7 + 6   14 − 5
☐ ◯ ☐

12 − 7   11 − 7
☐ ◯ ☐

Fruity Fun

Smart Start • EMC 9849 • © Evan-Moor Corp.

Count by 5s.

𝍸𝍸 𝍸𝍸 𝍸𝍸 𝍸𝍸 𝍸𝍸 𝍸𝍸 𝍸𝍸 𝍸𝍸 𝍸𝍸 𝍸𝍸

_____ _____ _____ _____ _____ _____ _____ _____ _____ _____

𝍸𝍸 𝍸𝍸 𝍸𝍸 𝍸𝍸 𝍸𝍸 𝍸𝍸 𝍸𝍸 𝍸𝍸 𝍸𝍸 𝍸𝍸

_____ _____ _____ _____ _____ _____ _____ _____ _____ _____

Add.

$$\begin{array}{r} 6 \\ 4 \\ +\ 3 \\ \hline \end{array} \qquad \begin{array}{r} 2 \\ 3 \\ +\ 1 \\ \hline \end{array} \qquad \begin{array}{r} 4 \\ 3 \\ +\ 5 \\ \hline \end{array} \qquad \begin{array}{r} 9 \\ 0 \\ +\ 4 \\ \hline \end{array} \qquad \begin{array}{r} 7 \\ 3 \\ +\ 6 \\ \hline \end{array}$$

Read the word. Fill in the circle under the number.

zero	eight	three
7 0 2	9 4 8	10 3 2
○ ○ ○	○ ○ ○	○ ○ ○

Color the Igloos

Find the answers. Color the igloos with **14** blue.

Color the igloos with **15 red**.

Color the igloos with **16 green**.

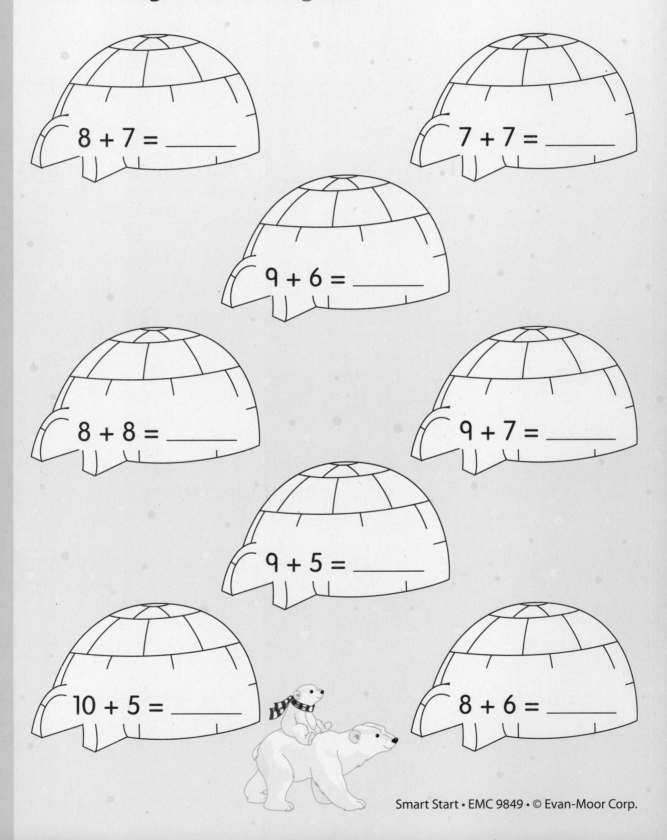

8 + 7 = _____

7 + 7 = _____

9 + 6 = _____

8 + 8 = _____

9 + 7 = _____

9 + 5 = _____

10 + 5 = _____

8 + 6 = _____

Smart Start • EMC 9849 • © Evan-Moor Corp.

Meet the Walrus Families

Skills:

Addition & Subtraction to 16

Use each family of numbers to make 2 addition problems and 2 subtraction problems.

9, 6, 15

_____ + _____ = _____

_____ + _____ = _____

_____ − _____ = _____

_____ − _____ = _____

7, 8, 15

_____ + _____ = _____

_____ + _____ = _____

_____ − _____ = _____

_____ − _____ = _____

9, 7, 16

_____ + _____ = _____

_____ + _____ = _____

_____ − _____ = _____

_____ − _____ = _____

8, 6, 14

_____ + _____ = _____

_____ + _____ = _____

_____ − _____ = _____

_____ − _____ = _____

Add or subtract.

$6 + 7 =$ _____ $13 − 6 =$ _____ $8 + 8 =$ _____

$7 + 6 =$ _____ $13 − 7 =$ _____ $16 − 8 =$ _____

Chilly Capers

Animals at the Poles

Note: You may need to help your child read the word problems.

Write the problems. Answer them.

9 penguins were swimming in the sea. 7 more penguins jumped in. How many penguins were swimming in the sea?

☐ + ☐ = ☐

There were _____ penguins swimming in the sea.

16 walruses were lying on the ice. 9 walruses slid back into the sea. How many walruses were still on the ice?

☐ − ☐ = ☐

There were _____ walruses still on the ice.

Polar Bear saw 6 seals in the morning and 9 seals in the afternoon. How many seals did Polar Bear see in all?

☐ + ☐ = ☐

Polar Bear saw _____ seals in all.

16 penguins were caught for the zoo. 8 of the penguins got away. How many penguins were left?

☐ − ☐ = ☐

There were _____ penguins left.

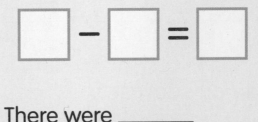

Smart Start • EMC 9849 • © Evan-Moor Corp.

Skills:

Reading
a Graph

Use the information from the graph to answer the questions.

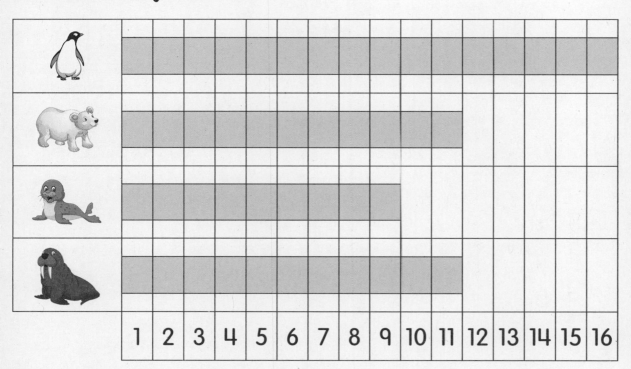

1. How many fish did each animal eat?

  _____    _____   _____

2. Which animal ate the most fish?

3. Which animal ate the fewest fish?

4. Polar Bear and Seal ate _____ fish in all.

5. Penguin ate _____ more fish than Walrus.

Find the Seal

Skills:

Addition &
Subtraction
to 16

Connect the answers in order from smallest to largest.

$$14 - 9$$

$$10 + 2$$

$$15 - 9$$

$$7 + 4$$

$$7 + 6$$

$$13 - 6$$

$$12 - 2$$

$$16 - 8$$

$$6 + 8$$

$$16 - 7$$

Chilly Capers

Write the time.

Skills:

Telling Time to
the Half Hour

_____ : _____

_____ : _____

_____ : _____

_____ : _____

_____ : _____

_____ : _____

_____ : _____

_____ : _____

_____ : _____

chilly capers

How Many Fish?

Circle the best **estimate**.

1   10

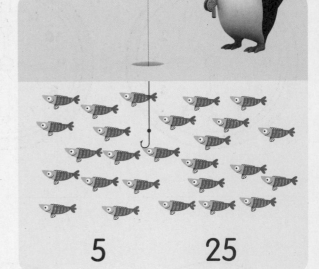

5   25

15   35

10   50

Count by 5s.

5, _____, _____, 20, _____, 30, _____, _____, _____, 50

Count by 10s.

10, _____, _____, 40, _____, _____, _____, 80 _____, _____

Smart Start • EMC 9849 • © Evan-Moor Corp.

TEST YOUR SKILLS

Add or subtract.

16 – 7 = _____   9 + 6 = _____   15 – 9 = _____

8 + 7 = _____   15 – 8 = _____   7 + 9 = _____

What's missing?

6, _____, 10, 12, _____

20, _____, 30, _____

_____, 80, 90, _____

What's missing?
Count by 1s.

_____, 30, _____, 32

49, _____, _____, 52

Julie saw 9 polar bears and 7 seals.
How many animals did Julie see in all?

Julie saw _____ animals in all.

Add or subtract.

$$\begin{array}{r} 47 \\ -\ 25 \\ \hline \end{array} \qquad \begin{array}{r} 29 \\ -\ 3 \\ \hline \end{array} \qquad \begin{array}{r} 56 \\ +\ 13 \\ \hline \end{array} \qquad \begin{array}{r} 13 \\ +\ 4 \\ \hline \end{array}$$

How much?

   _____ ¢

_____ : _____

_____ : _____

How many pins?
Circle the best estimate.

40 pins

20 pins

ASSESSMENT 8

Shapes

Match.

sphere   cube   cone

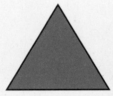  

Write the name of each shape.

At the circus

166

What's Missing?

MATH GAME

$7 +$ _____ $= 15$

$15 -$ _____ $= 9$

MATH GAME

$8 +$ _____ $= 16$

_____ $+ 9 = 16$

MATH GAME

_____ $- 9 = 9$

_____ $- 8 = 9$

MATH GAME

Write your own game.

_____ $+$ _____ $=$ _____

_____ $-$ _____ $=$ _____

At the Circus

A Day at the Circus

Note: You may need to help your child read the word problems.

Skills:

Word Problems: Addition & Subtraction to 18

There were 18 tigers. Sarah fed 9 of the tigers. How many tigers still need to be fed?

_____ tigers still need to be fed.

Alex saw 9 seals and 8 circus dogs. How many animals did Alex see in all?

Alex saw _____ animals in all.

Abe ate 9 bags of peanuts and 5 bags of popcorn while watching the circus. How many bags of food did Abe eat in all?

Abe ate _____ bags of food in all.

There were 16 clowns. 7 of the clowns were riding a unicycle. The rest of the clowns were walking. How many clowns were walking?

There were _____ clowns walking.

Smart Start • EMC 9849 • © Evan-Moor Corp.

At the Circus

Skills:

Fractions

Greater Than,
Less Than

Name the fractions.
Write **>** or **<** in the circles.

$\frac{1}{3}$ < $\frac{3}{4}$

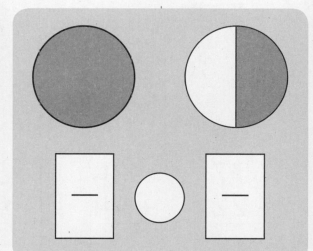

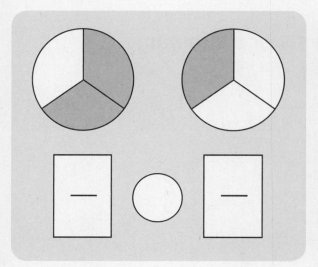

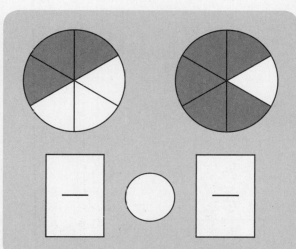

Color to show the fraction.

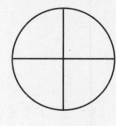
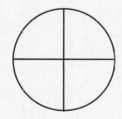

$\frac{1}{3}$ $\frac{1}{4}$ $\frac{2}{4}$ $\frac{2}{3}$

At the Circus

Add and Subtract Tens and Ones

Remember: Add the ones first.

tens	ones
3	1
+ 2	8
5	9

$$23 + 72$$ $$54 + 15$$ $$11 + 38$$ $$15 + 84$$

$$77 + 22$$ $$34 + 44$$ $$50 + 49$$ $$25 + 63$$ $$45 + 41$$

How many of your answers were the same? _____

tens	ones
8	7
− 6	5
2	2

$$99 - 87$$ $$45 - 20$$ $$76 - 43$$ $$48 - 16$$

$$79 - 44$$ $$80 - 40$$ $$79 - 55$$ $$87 - 10$$ $$38 - 0$$

How many of your answers had three **tens**? _____

Smart Start • EMC 9849 • © Evan-Moor Corp.

Skills:

Number Words

Place Value—
Tens & Ones

Read the word. Write the number.

ten _____   four _____   eight _____

six _____   one _____   seven _____

Write the number word.

6 _____   10 _____   7 _____

Write the number.

_____ tens and _____ ones = _____

_____

_____ tens and _____ ones = _____

_____

_____ tens and _____ ones = _____

At the Circus

Add and subtract.

```
  23        11        56
+ 72      + 38      + 31
```

```
  99        50        46
- 73      - 30      - 43
```

Match the fraction.

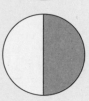

$$\frac{1}{2}$$

$$\frac{1}{4}$$

$$\frac{1}{3}$$

Fill in the circle for the correct time.

○ 2:00   ○ 12:00

○ 8:30   ○ 9:30

○ 12:00   ○ 10:00

○ 1:30   ○ 6:30

Math

_____

Name

I practiced addition, subtraction, telling time, fractions, and many other math skills.

I did activities that helped me get ready to learn more math skills!

_____

Date

Science Concepts and Basic Skills

Helping Your Child Learn About Science

Science is all around us, and children are naturally curious about their world. They investigate, problem solve, experiment, and imagine new ways to do things— they are, by nature, scientists! Studies show that children learn best through hands-on experiences. As your child asks questions about the world, you may look to science to answer some of those questions. The activities in this section will help you connect your child's real-world experiences to science concepts and vocabulary.

Reading Selections

Read the selection to your child. Point to vocabulary words and have your child say each word aloud. Discuss how the illustrations or photos relate to the science concept. Then, if your child is able, have him or her read the selection to you.

Visual Literacy

Illustrations and photos help your child relate science concepts to the real-world. Use the visual literacy activities to reinforce the science concepts that were presented in the reading selection. Provide your child with support by reading the directions aloud and answering any questions he or she may have about the activity.

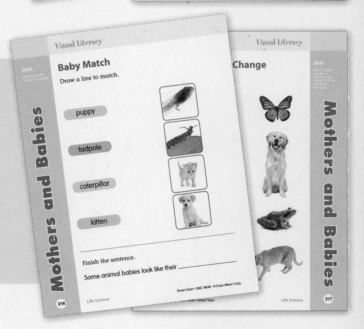

Vocabulary

The vocabulary activities range from word puzzles to writing vocabulary words to complete sentences. Provide your child with support by reading the directions aloud and answering any questions he or she may have about the activity.

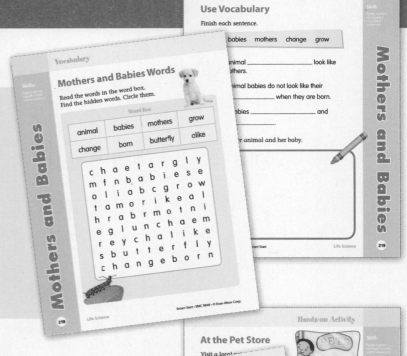

Hands-on Activities

The hands-on activities provide your child with opportunities to connect science concepts to the real world. The activities focus on developing process skills such as observing and collecting and organizing information. In addition, you and your child will create projects that bring science concepts to life. These activities are designed for parents and children to complete together.

Certificates

After your child completes each science domain, remove the certificate from the book and have your child write his or her name on it. Congratulate your child on a job well done and post the certificate in a prominent place.

Concept:

There are different sources of light.

Light

Light is all around us.

Some light comes from nature.

sun

moon

stars

Some light comes from things that people make.

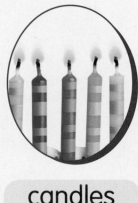
candles

flashlight

lamp

Smart Start • EMC 9849 • © Evan-Moor Corp.

Light helps us see.
If we did not have light,
the world would be dark.

Light helps us live.
People, animals, and
plants need light.

Light

Light Match

Draw a line to match.

candle

sun

lamp

moon

Finish the sentence.

Light helps us _____.

Physical Science

Who Makes It?

Look at the picture. Check the correct box.

Skill:

Match graphic images to science concepts

nature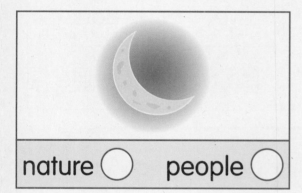

people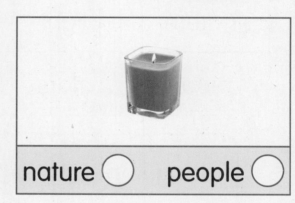

nature ◯   people ◯

nature ◯   people ◯

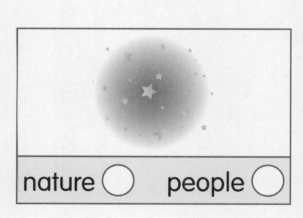

nature ◯   people ◯

nature ◯   people ◯

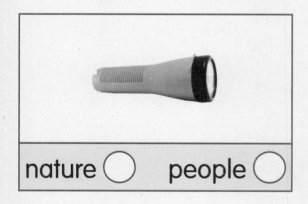

nature ◯   people ◯

nature ◯   people ◯

Light Words

Read the words in the word box.
Find the hidden words. Circle them.

Word Box

nature	light	live	dark
moon	stars	lamp	candle

```
l  i  n  d  m  o  o  n  k  a
f  g  c  e  s  d  l  h  n  l
e  l  a  m  p  o  i  s  g  i
c  h  n  a  t  u  r  e  t  v
a  t  r  k  i  d  m  f  s  e
n  a  l  i  g  h  t  e  l  k
d  g  s  f  v  i  n  t  d  a
l  n  d  a  r  k  d  v  e  o
e  l  a  o  b  s  t  a  r  s
```

Use Vocabulary

Finish each sentence.

| light | nature | live |

1. Some light comes from _____.

2. If we did not have _____, the world would be dark.

3. Light helps us _____.

Draw light that comes from nature.

Physical Science

Lights Inside

Your house has light from things that people made. Draw four lights that people made and write the names.

Physical Science

Smart Start • EMC 9849 • © Evan-Moor Corp.

Lights Outside

You can see light from nature outside. Draw three sources of light from nature and write the names.

Skill:

Apply science concepts to real-world situations

Light

Physical Science

Concept:

Shadows are produced when a light source is blocked.

Light and Shadows

Light moves in a line.

Light can move through some things.

Light moves through glass.

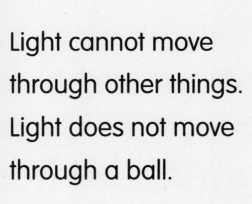

Light cannot move
through other things.
Light does not move
through a ball.

When light cannot move through something,
you may see a shadow .

A shadow is a dark spot.

Skill:

Match graphic
images to words

Shadow Match

Draw a line to match.

shadow

glass

light

Finish the sentence.

When light cannot move through something,

it makes a _____.

Shadows

What Made the Shadow?

Draw a line to match.

© Evan-Moor Corp. • EMC 9849 • Smart Start

Shadows

Physical Science

189

Shadow and Light Words

Read the words in the word box.
Find the hidden words. Circle them.

Word Box

shadow	light	glass	dark
through	shine	line	move

```
d  r  k  o  u  m  g  l  s  i
a  s  h  a  d  o  w  n  e  d
l  g  t  n  u  v  r  t  c  a
i  s  h  i  n  e  k  h  v  r
g  a  r  t  h  o  n  r  u  k
h  e  g  l  a  s  s  o  r  t
t  a  c  h  r  o  k  u  d  l
s  l  i  n  e  v  d  g  o  e
t  o  w  d  h  i  t  h  e  k
```

Shadows

Use Vocabulary

Skill:

Apply science vocabulary in context sentences

Finish each sentence.

light	line	shadow

1. Light moves in a _____.

2. _____ cannot move through some things.

3. A _____ is a dark spot.

Draw an object or person that has a shadow.

Shadow Art

Create a picture that has a shadow.

What You Need

- black, white, and light-colored construction paper
- crayons
- scissors
- glue

What You Do

1 Draw a picture of an object or person on the white paper.

2 Put the black piece of paper behind the white paper. Hold both pieces of paper together as you cut out your drawing.

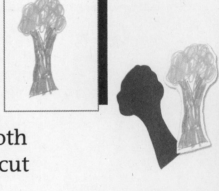

3 Draw a sun on the light-colored construction paper. Glue your drawing onto the paper. Glue the shadow onto the paper.

4 Write a sentence that tells what the picture shows.

Shadows

Physical Science

Shadow Walk

Go outside and find shadows.

Skill:

Make scientific observations and record information

What You Need

- a camera

What You Do

1 On a sunny day, get a camera and go for a walk.

2 Look for shadows outside. When you see a shadow, take a picture of it.

3 After you get home, look through your pictures and answer the questions below.

Draw and write to answer the questions.

1. What shadow did you like best? Draw it.

2. What did it show? _____

3. Why was there a shadow? _____

_____

Shadows

Physical Science

PHYSICAL SCIENCE

HOORAY! I DID IT!

_____
Name

I read about light and shadows.

I learned that light and shadows are part of the world around me.

I did activities that helped me better understand and talk about physical science in my world.

Concept:

Leaves help trees survive and grow.

All Kinds of Leaves

Leaves help trees grow and live.
Trees grow leaves of many shapes
and sizes.

Leaves

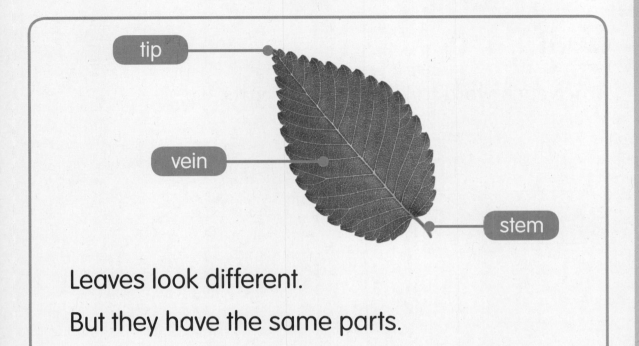

Leaves look different.

But they have the same parts.

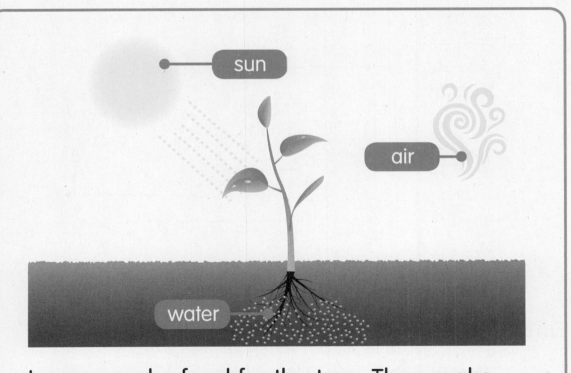

Leaves make food for the tree. They make food from the sun, air, and water.

Life Science

Leaves

Skill:

Label graphic images to demonstrate understanding of science concepts

Leaf Parts

Trace each word to label the leaf parts.

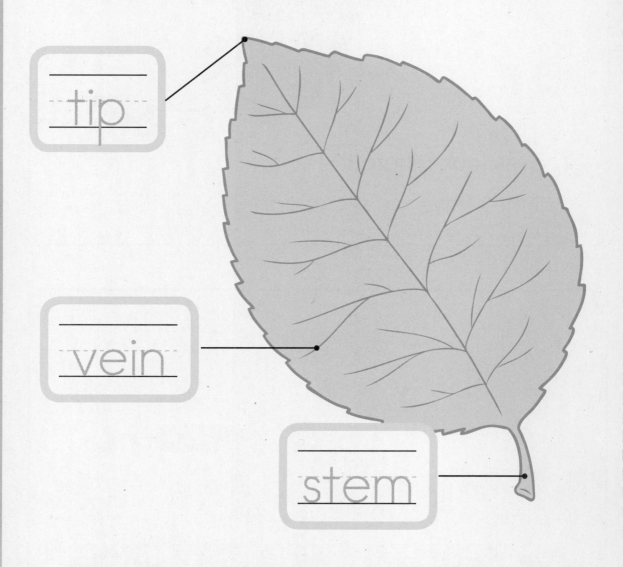

tip

vein

stem

....

Finish the sentence.

Leaves help trees grow and _____.

Leaves

Smart Start • EMC 9849 • © Evan-Moor Corp.

Leaves Have Shapes

Draw a line to match.

Skill:
Visual
discrimination

Leaf Words

Unscramble the words about leaves.
Write the words in the boxes.

Word Box

tip	leaf	tree	sizes
leaves	live	shapes	grow

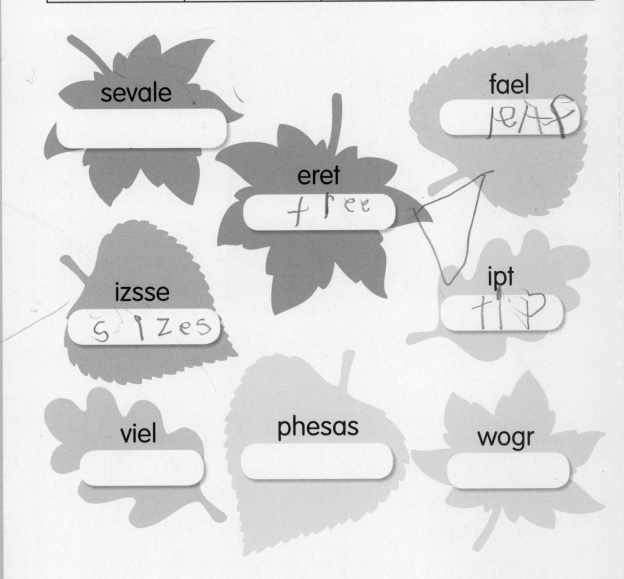

sevale

fael

leaf

eret

tree

izsse

sizes

ipt

tip

viel

phesas

wogr

Leaves

Use Vocabulary

Skill:

Apply science vocabulary in context sentences

Finish each sentence.

trees	live	food

1. Leaves help trees grow and _____.

2. _____ grow leaves of many shapes and sizes.

3. Leaves make _____ for the tree.

Draw your favorite leaf.

[drawing box]

Leaves

Leaf Rubbings

Use real leaves to make a picture!

What You Need

- paper bag
- leaves of different shapes and sizes
- crayons with wrappers removed
- paper

What You Do

1 Take the paper bag outdoors and collect leaves of different shapes, sizes, and colors.

2 On a hard, flat surface, place a leaf bottom side up on a piece of paper.

3 Put another sheet of paper on top of the leaf.

4 Rub the side of a crayon gently on the area over the leaf. Try to keep the leaf in place with one hand while you color with the other hand.

5 Do the same thing using other crayon colors and leaves.

6 Play with making patterns or your own "tree" of leaves.

Leaves

Life Science

Animals and Eggs

Babies in Eggs

Some animals lay eggs. Their babies grow inside until they are ready to hatch.

bird

turtle

spider

snake

Animals with feathers, scales, or slippery skin lay eggs in many places.

Parents take care of their babies.

They feed them and keep them safe.

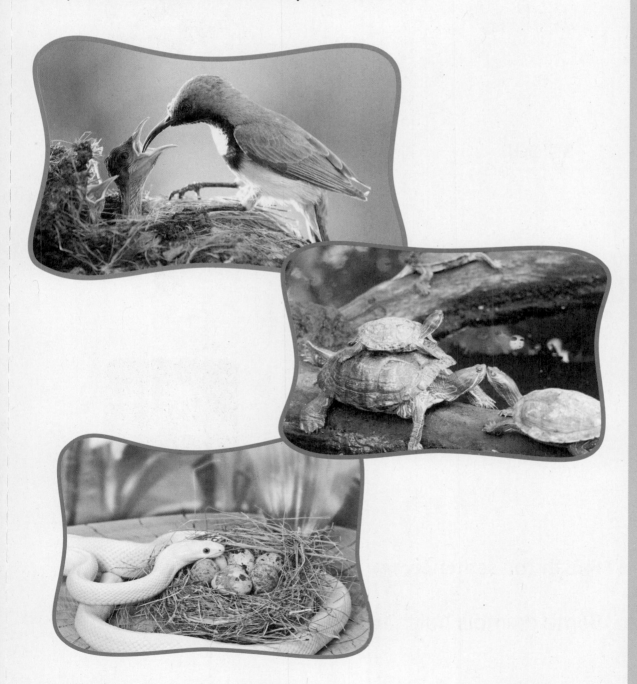

Egg Match

Draw a line to match.

turtle

spider

bird

snake

Finish the sentence.

Some animals hatch from _____.

Life Science

Animals and Eggs

Skill:
Label graphic
images to
demonstrate
understanding
of science
concepts

A Life Cycle

Number the pictures to match.

1. The egg is laid.

2. The egg hatches.

3. The baby is fed.

4. The baby is kept safe.

Animals and Eggs

Egg Words

Unscramble the words about eggs.
Write the words in the boxes.

Word Box

eggs	hatch	animals	babies
parents	feed	safe	lay

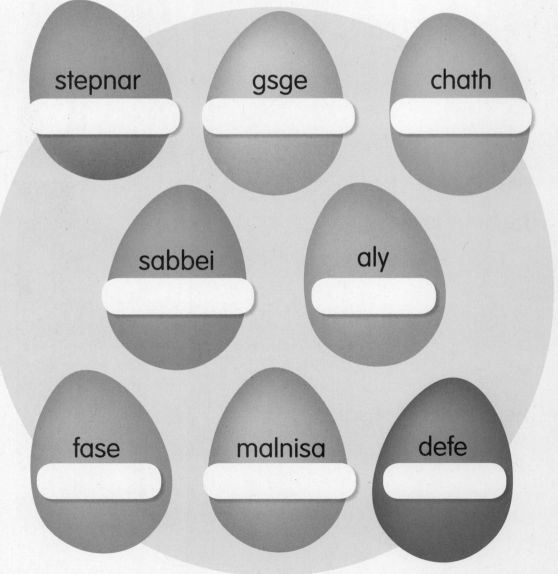

stepnar

gsge

chath

sabbei

aly

fase

malnisa

defe

Life Science

Smart Start • EMC 9849 • © Evan-Moor Corp.

Animals and Eggs

Skills:

Read science words; Visual discrimination

Use Vocabulary

Skill:

Apply science vocabulary in context sentences

Finish each sentence.

parents	eggs	hatch

1. Some animals lay _____.

2. Babies grow in the eggs until they _____.

3. _____ take care of their babies.

Draw an animal and its eggs.

Animals and Eggs

What's Hatching Book

Make a book about animals that hatch from eggs!

What You Need

- scissors
- stapler
- crayons, colored pencils, or markers
- 3 sheets of white paper
- 1 sheet of construction paper

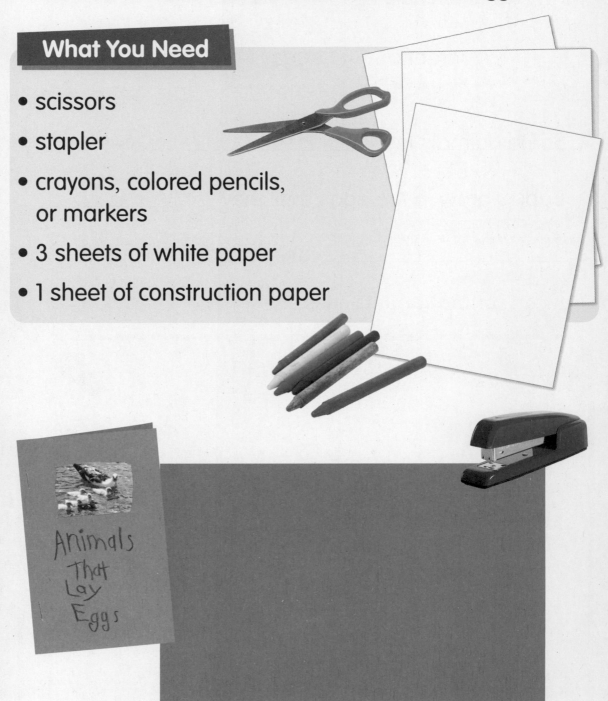

Skill:

Make art projects to represent science concepts

Animals and Eggs

Smart Start • EMC 9849 • © Evan-Moor Corp.

What You Do

1 Think about the animals that lay eggs.

2 Look at the pictures of the animals on pages 48–51 of this book.

3 Fold the sheets of white paper and construction paper in half. Staple the folded edge to make a book.

4 Cut out, from a magazine, a photo of an animal that lays eggs. Glue it to the cover of your book. Write a title for your book.

5 On each page of the book, draw a picture of an animal next to its baby hatching from an egg.

6 Write a sentence below each picture you draw.

7 Read your book to someone.

Animals and Eggs

Concept:

Some animal babies look like their mothers, but others do not.

Mothers and Babies

Mothers and Babies

Some animal babies look
a lot like their mothers.

They have the same body parts.
They are the same color.
They are the same shape.

dog

puppy

Some babies do not look like
their mothers when they are born.
They look different.

butterfly

caterpillar

Life Science

But they will grow and change.

One day, they will look like their mothers, too.

tadpole

froglet

frog

Baby Match

Draw a line to match.

puppy

tadpole

caterpillar

kitten

Mothers and Babies

Finish the sentence.

Some animal babies look like their _____.

Animals Grow and Change

Draw a line to match.

Skill:

Match graphic images to demonstrate understanding of science concepts

Mothers and Babies

Mothers and Babies Words

Read the words in the word box.
Find the hidden words. Circle them.

Word Box

animal	babies	mothers	grow
change	born	butterfly	alike

```
c h a e t a r g l y
m f n b a b i e s e
o l i a b c g r o w
t a m o r i k e a l
h r a b r m o t n i
e g l u n c h a e m
r e y c h a l i k e
s b u t t e r f l y
c h a n g e b o r n
```

Mothers and Babies

Use Vocabulary

Finish each sentence.

| babies | mothers | change | grow |

1. Some animal _____ look like their mothers.

2. Some animal babies do not look like their _____ when they are born.

3. Animal babies _____ and _____.

Draw a mother animal and her baby.

Mothers and Babies

Mothers and Babies

Mother and Baby

Draw a picture of a mother and her baby.

What You Need

- paper
- crayons or colored pencils

What You Do

1 Choose an animal mother and baby to draw.

2 Draw a picture of the animal mother and her baby.

3 Write a sentence that tells how they are alike or different.

4 Show your picture to someone and explain how they are alike or different.

mother   baby

The mother has wings and the baby has legs.

At the Pet Store

Visit a local pet store to see tadpoles and frogs.

Skill:

Apply science concepts to real-world situations

Draw pictures of what you saw.

Tadpole	Frog

Write about what you saw.

_____

_____

_____

Mothers and Babies

LIFE SCIENCE

HOORAY!

I DID IT!

_____
Name

I read about leaves, animals and eggs, and mothers and babies.

I learned that all of these things are part of the world around me.

I did activities that helped me better understand and talk about life science in my world.

Geography Skills and Concepts

Helping Your Child Learn About Geography

Children see landforms and bodies of water in their everyday lives. They may know what a mountain is, but they may not know what makes it different from a hill. They may know what a lake is, but they may not know what makes it different from an ocean. These activities will help your child learn about landforms, bodies of water, and maps.

Geography Activities and Minibook

Read the directions to your child and provide support as your child completes the map activity.

Guide your child as he or she cuts apart the pages and staples them to make the *Landforms and Bodies of Water* minibook. After your child writes his or her name on the book, read it together. Talk about the landforms and bodies of water in your area or in places that you've visited.

Geography Cards

Cut apart the geography cards. Then use them to play the matching games below.

Game 1: Place the cards on a flat surface with the pictures and words facing up. Have your child match the definitions to the pictures to make a pair.

Game 2: Mix up the cards. Then place the cards on a flat surface, pictures and words facing down. Have your child turn over two cards and see if the definition matches the picture. If the cards do not match, turn them back over and try again. Continue playing until all the cards are matched.

Certificate

After your child completes the geography section of this book, remove the geography certificate and have your child write his or her name on it. Congratulate your child on a job well done and post the certificate in a prominent place.

Places on a Map

A map is a drawing of a place from above.
A map shows where things are.

▶ This map shows a town.

▶ Look at the map. Write the words to complete the sentences.

1. The school is on _____ Avenue.

2. You go into the gas station from _____ Street.

3. Kari and Kim live on _____ Avenue.

4. Brown Street is between the school and the _____.

5. Green Street and _____ Street go by the park.

Landforms and Bodies of Water

A landform is a shape of land.
Earth has many kinds of landforms.
Earth has many different bodies of water, too.

Let's look at some of them.

Name _____

1

A **mountain** is a very high raised area of land. Sometimes it has snow at the top.

• Point to the top of the mountain.

A **hill** is a raised area of land.
It is lower and smaller than
a mountain.

• Draw a small tree on the hill.

3

An **island** is land with
water all around it.
You can find many islands
in the ocean.

• Draw a tree on the island.

4

A **volcano** is a mountain that has an opening. Lava, gas, and ash can erupt through the opening.

• Does the lava look hot or cold?

5

A **desert** is a dry and sandy or rocky area. There is very little rainfall. There are only a few plants.

• Draw a rattlesnake in the desert.

6

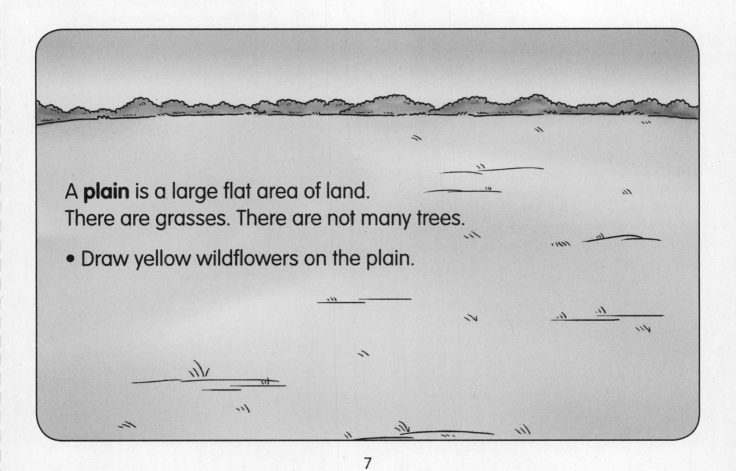

A **plain** is a large flat area of land. There are grasses. There are not many trees.

• Draw yellow wildflowers on the plain.

7

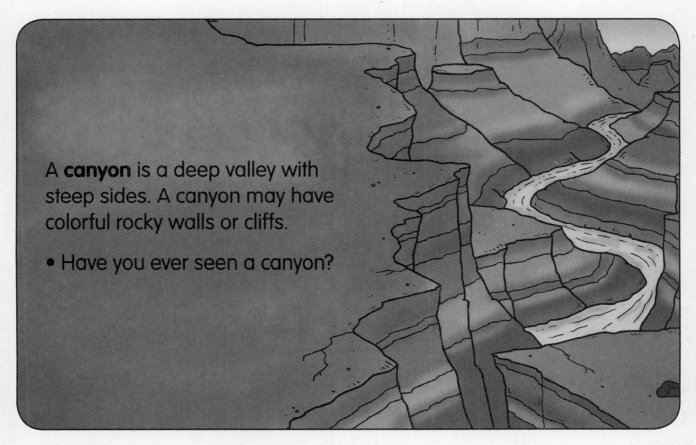

A **canyon** is a deep valley with steep sides. A canyon may have colorful rocky walls or cliffs.

• Have you ever seen a canyon?

8

A **valley** is low land between hills or mountains. Valleys can be narrow or they can be miles wide.

• Draw a deer in the valley.

9

An **ocean** is a large body of salt water. Earth has five oceans. They are named the Atlantic, Arctic, Indian, Pacific, and Southern.

• Draw a ship on the ocean.

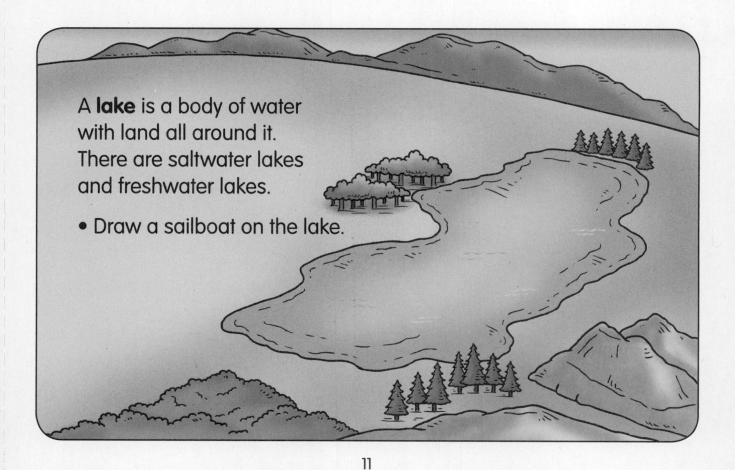

A **lake** is a body of water with land all around it. There are saltwater lakes and freshwater lakes.

• Draw a sailboat on the lake.

11

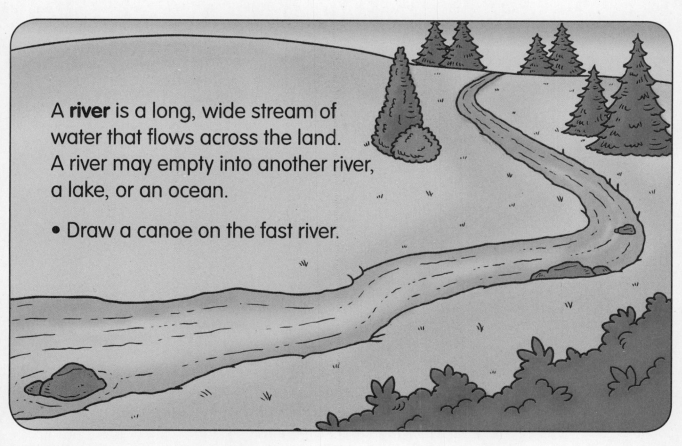

A **river** is a long, wide stream of water that flows across the land. A river may empty into another river, a lake, or an ocean.

• Draw a canoe on the fast river.

Landforms and Bodies of Water
Card Match

Cut out the cards. Match the cards.

**Landforms and
Bodies of Water**
Card Match

Smart Start • EMC 9849 • © Evan-Moor Corp.

**Landforms and
Bodies of Water**
Card Match

Smart Start • EMC 9849 • © Evan-Moor Corp.

**Landforms and
Bodies of Water**
Card Match

Smart Start • EMC 9849 • © Evan-Moor Corp.

**Landforms and
Bodies of Water**
Card Match

Smart Start • EMC 9849 • © Evan-Moor Corp.

**Landforms and
Bodies of Water**
Card Match

Smart Start • EMC 9849 • © Evan-Moor Corp.

**Landforms and
Bodies of Water**
Card Match

Smart Start • EMC 9849 • © Evan-Moor Corp.

island
An island is land with water all around it.

canyon
A canyon is a deep valley with steep sides.

mountain
A mountain is a very high raised area of land.

lake
A lake is a large body of water with land all around it.

volcano
A volcano is a mountain with an opening.

desert
A desert is a dry and sandy or rocky area.

Landforms and
Bodies of Water
Card Match

Smart Start • EMC 9849 • © Evan-Moor Corp.

Landforms and
Bodies of Water
Card Match

Smart Start • EMC 9849 • © Evan-Moor Corp.

Landforms and
Bodies of Water
Card Match

Smart Start • EMC 9849 • © Evan-Moor Corp.

Landforms and
Bodies of Water
Card Match

Smart Start • EMC 9849 • © Evan-Moor Corp.

Landforms and
Bodies of Water
Card Match

Smart Start • EMC 9849 • © Evan-Moor Corp.

Landforms and
Bodies of Water
Card Match

Smart Start • EMC 9849 • © Evan-Moor Corp.

Geography

_____
Name

I learned that there are many different types of landforms and bodies of water.

I did activities that helped me identify landforms and bodies of water and locate places on a map.

_____
Date

You Completed the Section
GOOD WORK!

Helping Your Child Be a Critical Thinker

Critical thinking comes naturally to young children. They learn autonomy through exploration, observe their environment using logic and reasoning, try new things, and think creatively. As children grow and enter an academic setting, some of their natural curiosity and problem-solving instincts are not engaged as often as they could be. The activities in this section will encourage your child to "think about his or her thinking" through creative, analytical, and evaluative tasks.

Read All About It

Read the selection to your child. Discuss how the illustrations and photos relate to the topic. Then, if your child is able, have him or her read the selection to you. After reading the selection, discuss how the topic relates to your child's life.

Tell What You Know

The activities on these pages provide opportunities for children to connect their knowledge and opinions to the topic. Encourage your child to think about his or her experiences and support his or her curiosity by discussing the questions and topics together.

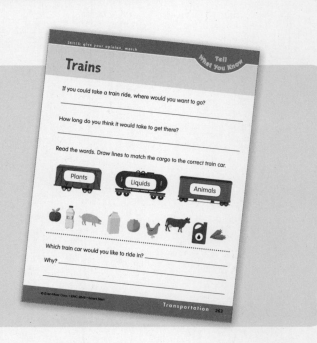

Critical Thinking Activities

The critical thinking activities are designed to engage children in application, analysis, synthesis, and evaluation tasks. The cross-curricular activities present science, math, social studies, and language arts content.

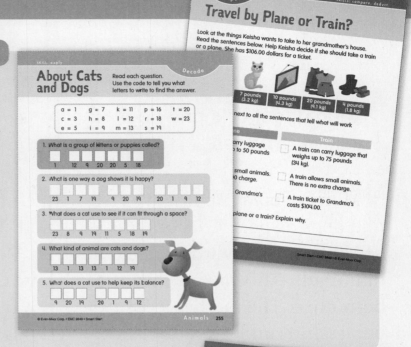

Art Projects and Hands-on Activities

The art projects and hands-on activities provide children with opportunities to use critical thinking skills to create. Encourage your child to tap into his or her creativity and innovation and to have fun with the hands-on activities. After your child completes each project, discuss the steps taken to create it. Encourage your child to explain what he or she enjoyed most and why.

Certificate

After your child completes the thinking skills section of this book, remove the certificate from the book and have your child write his or her name on it. Congratulate your child on a job well done and post the certificate in a prominent place.

Cats and Dogs

Read about cats and dogs. Then answer the questions on the following pages.

Many people like to have cats and dogs as pets. Cats and dogs are alike in many ways. They are mammals. This means they are born alive. The mother feeds her babies with milk from her body. Puppies and kittens cannot see or

their food. Dogs can hear very well. They hear better than people do. Dogs can learn to do many kinds of work to help people.

Cats have been pets for thousands of years, too. Cats use their sharp teeth to hold their

do many things when they are born. About two weeks after they are born, they can see and are strong enough to do more things.

Both cats and dogs have four legs and fur or hair. They both have sharp claws and teeth, too.

Dogs have been pets for about 15,000 years. Some dogs are very large. Some are very small. They have smooth tongues and sharp teeth. The teeth help them to eat

food. They use their rough tongues to clean their fur. A cat's long tail helps it to keep its balance. Cats meow, purr, and hiss to show how they feel.

If you have a pet dog or cat, then you know that you must take care of it. Pets need a safe, warm place to sleep. They need good food and water. They need to spend time with you. Dogs and cats make wonderful pet friends.

Cats and Dogs

Which do you like better, **cats** or **dogs**? _____

Why? _____

Write 3 <u>different</u> words that describe **cats**.

1. _____

2. _____

3. _____

Which kitten does <u>not</u> belong?

Write 3 <u>different</u> words that describe **dogs**.

1. _____

2. _____

3. _____

Which does <u>not</u> belong?

Categorize

Our Four-Legged Friends

Read each numbered item below. Does it tell about **cats**, **dogs**, or **both**?
Write the number where it belongs in the Venn diagram.
Then make up 3 items of your own. Write those numbers, too.

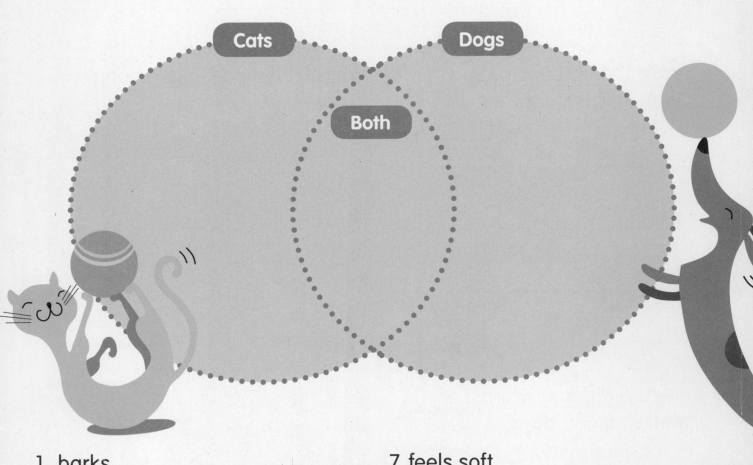

1. barks

2. has whiskers

3. purrs

4. has a tail

5. has sharp teeth

6. likes to fetch

7. feels soft

8. climbs trees

9. can be trained to sit

10. _____

11. _____

12. _____

The Iditarod

Solve

Read each sentence.
Color the squares to move each dog as it says.
Find out which dog wins the race.

 Hotfoot

 Stormy

 Nugget

 Digger

Finish Line

1. Hotfoot, Digger, and Stormy get a head start. Move them forward one.

2. Digger stops to dig a hole. Hotfoot and Stormy move ahead one.

3. Nugget is coming! Move him ahead one.

4. Hotfoot stops to scratch his ear. Move Stormy ahead one.

5. Digger and Nugget dig in. Move them ahead two.

6. Stormy gets nervous. Move ahead one.

7. Hotfoot smells a rabbit. He doesn't move.

8. Nugget sees the finish. Move ahead two.

9. Digger catches up with Stormy.

10. Stormy stops to snap at Digger. Digger rushes ahead two.

The Iditarod Sled Dog Race is run every winter in Alaska. The dogs run 1,000 miles through snow and ice.

The winner is: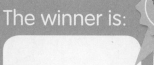

Compare

Twins

Which 2 dogs are exactly alike?
Mark the twins.

Smart Start • EMC 9849 • © Evan-Moor Corp.

Draw

My Cat

Follow the directions to draw a cat.
Then color your cat and complete the sentences.

My cat's name is _____.

It lives _____.

It likes to _____.

Dog Facts

Unscramble the word to finish each dog fact.

1. Dogs mostly sweat from the bottoms of their **tefe**.

2. Dalmatians are born all **tihwe**. No spots!

3. One special kind of dog has webbed feet to help it **msiw**.

4. Not all dogs shed their **ruf** in the summer.

5. Some dogs can **nru** up to 42 miles per hour.

6. All puppies are born **dlinb**. They will begin to see and hear at about two weeks old.

About Cats and Dogs

Read each question.
Use the code to tell you what
letters to write to find the answer.

a = 1	g = 7	k = 11	p = 16	t = 20
c = 3	h = 8	l = 12	r = 18	w = 23
e = 5	i = 9	m = 13	s = 19	

1. **What is a group of kittens or puppies called?**

  1   12   9   20   20   5   18

2. **What is one way a dog shows it is happy?**

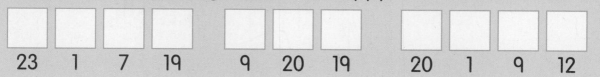

  23 1 7 19   9 20 19   20 1 9 12

3. **What does a cat use to see if it can fit through a space?**

  23 8 9 19 11 5 18 19

4. **What kind of animal are cats and dogs?**

  13 1 13 13 1 12 19

5. **What does a cat use to help keep its balance?**

  9 20 19   20 1 9 12

Compute

Cat Math

Read the word problem.
Solve and show your work.

Raymond has a pet cat. His cat eats 5 spoonfuls of cat food each day. How many spoonfuls of cat food will Raymond's cat eat in a 7-day week?

Work Space:

Answer: _____ spoonfuls

Raymond's cat had 6 kittens. He wants to sell the kittens for $4.00 each. How much money will he earn if he sells all the kittens?

Work Space:

Answer: $_____

Raymond's cat eats 1 can of cat food each day. Each can of cat food costs 50¢. How much money will Raymond spend on cat food in one week?

Work Space:

Answer: $_____

Raymond's cat sleeps 16 hours every day. How many hours is Raymond's cat awake each day?

Work Space:

Answer: _____ hours

Smart Start • EMC 9849 • © Evan-Moor Corp.

Which Cats?

Read the word problem.
Complete the list.

A   B   C   D

Janice wants to buy two kittens from Raymond.
Janice is not sure which two kittens she wants to
buy. She started to list all the different combinations
of 2 kittens that she could buy. Complete her list.

A and B		
A and C		

How many different combinations did you make?

Solve

Furry Friends Maze

Help the dog find his furry friend.

Smart Start • EMC 9849 • © Evan-Moor Corp.

Create

My Pup!

Read and follow the directions on page 260.

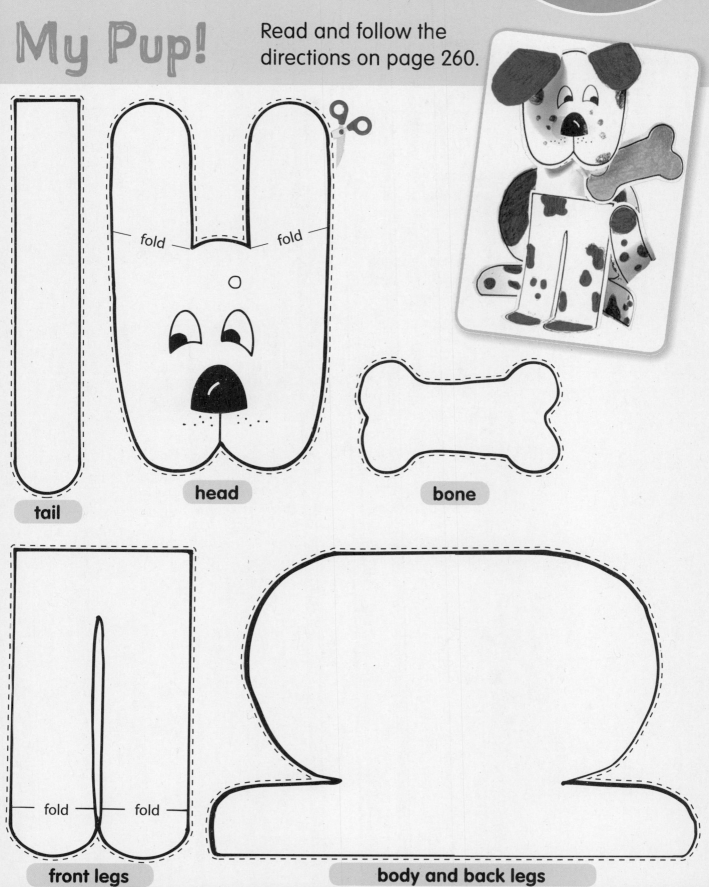

tail

fold   fold

head

bone

fold   fold

front legs

body and back legs

Paper Tube Pup directions:

1. Cover a toilet paper tube with white paper.

2. Remove page 259 from the book.

3. Color the dog patterns. Cut them out.

4. Glue the head and front legs to the front of the tube.

5. Glue the body and back legs to the back of the tube.

6. Glue the tail to the back of the body.

7. Glue the bone under the dog's mouth.

8. Set your Paper Tube Pup in place on page 261. Write about your pup!

tail

head

bone

front legs

body and back legs

My Pup!

Wag, beg, bark, and lick.
Run, dig, fetch a stick.

That's my pup!

Place your
Paper Tube Pup
friend here.

Write about your pup.

_____

_____

_____

_____

_____

_____

_____

_____

Facts About Planes and Trains

Long ago, people traveled on horses or in wagons. The trip would take weeks. Today, we can travel by trains and planes. It takes a few days to cross the United States by train. It takes only hours to fly across the country on a plane.

Trains and planes carry both passengers and cargo. Passengers are the people traveling. Items belonging to people or businesses are called cargo. Some trains and planes carry only passengers or only cargo. Some carry both.

Trains leave from stations. They travel along tracks. Planes leave from airports. They fly through the air.

Some trains go all the way across country, but some are used only in cities. These local trains take people around town to their jobs, to visit other people, or to shop.

Train tracks can be above ground or underground. Underground trains are called subways.

There are large planes and small planes. Some families and businesses have small planes. They may be used for fun or to fly people to meetings. Some small planes are used to spray farm fields to help the crops. Large planes are usually owned by airline companies. They fly many people from place to place. Large jets carry passengers or cargo long distances.

Have you ever traveled by train or plane? Where did you go? Did you enjoy your trip? Is there a place you'd like to go? Will you take a train or plane to get there?

Trains

If you could take a train ride, where would you want to go?

_____

How long do you think it would take to get there?

_____

Read the words. Draw lines to match the cargo to the correct train car.

Plants

Liquids

Animals

Which train car would you like to ride in? _____

Why? _____

_____

Planes

Write a sentence that is true about airplanes.

_____

Write a sentence that is <u>not</u> true about airplanes.

_____

Which one does <u>not</u> belong?
Write why.

_____

_____

_____

What is wrong with this picture?

_____

_____

What is something else that can fly? _____

Train Ride

You are riding on a train. What do you see out the window?

In the country	At the station

Get the train to the station.

Use a **blue** crayon to draw the path that takes the train through 3 tunnels to get to the station.

Use a **red** crayon to draw a path that takes the train through just 1 tunnel to get to the station.

Compare

A Plane

How is a plane like a **bird**?

_____

How is a plane like a **train**?

_____

You are riding in an airplane. Draw what you see out the window.

Write the opposite.

up _____

high _____

fast _____

take off _____

Where would you like to go on an airplane? Why?

_____

_____

Find

Plane Words

Circle each airplane word in the puzzle.

Word Box

wings   window

pilot   airport

tail   engine

seat   cockpit

```
c o c k p i t p
s e a t m w r d
p w e n g i n e
i p t w i n g s
l g a x c d z r
o a i r p o r t
t h l q k w b v
```

Circle things that an airplane needs to fly.

engine   seat   wings   window   pilot

Compute

Math Problems

There are 379 students in school. Only 261 ride the train. How many students don't ride the train?

Work Space:

_____ students

It is 10 miles from Tamara's house to school. She rides a train to school and back every day.

1. How many miles does she ride in one day?

2. How many miles does she ride in five days?

Work Space:

_____ miles in one day

_____ miles in five days

- 300 students never ride the train
- 64 students ride the train every day
- 111 ride the train sometimes

How many students ride the train?

Work Space:

_____ students

Train Shapes

Make 5 more trains by drawing the shapes in a different order each time.

Compare

Just Alike

Find the 2 airplanes that are alike.

Delivering Fresh Food

Fresh Foods Truck Company uses a pie chart to record the fruits and vegetables they deliver to each house. Here is their delivery to Mr. Phan's house. Use the pie chart to answer the questions. Each ◿ = 1.

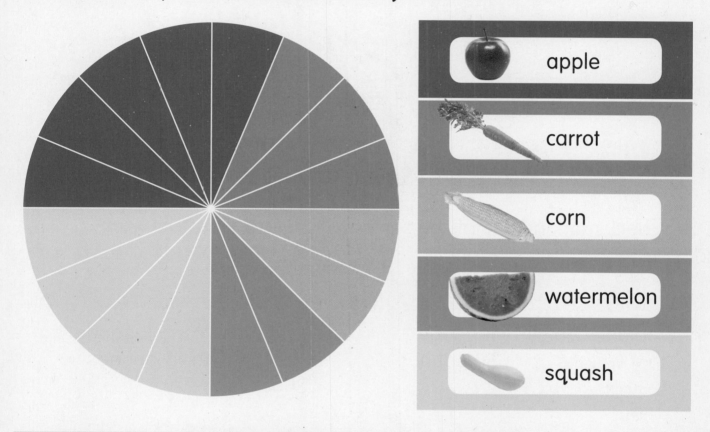

apple

carrot

corn

watermelon

squash

1. How many ears of corn were delivered?

_____

2. Which food did they deliver the most of?

_____

3. How many more carrots than watermelons were delivered?

_____

4. Which food was $\frac{1}{4}$ of the total amount delivered to Mr. Phan?

_____

Compute

Travel by Plane or Train?

Look at the things Keisha wants to take to her grandmother's house. Read the sentences below. Help Keisha decide if she should take a train or a plane. She has $106.00 dollars for a ticket.

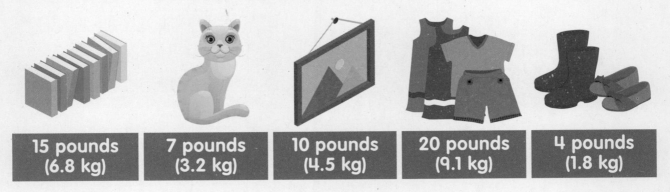

| 15 pounds (6.8 kg) | 7 pounds (3.2 kg) | 10 pounds (4.5 kg) | 20 pounds (9.1 kg) | 4 pounds (1.8 kg) |

Put a check mark next to all the sentences that tell what will work for Keisha.

Plane	Train
☐ A plane can carry luggage that weighs up to 50 pounds (23 kg).	☐ A train can carry luggage that weighs up to 75 pounds (34 kg).
☐ A plane allows small animals. There is a $25.00 charge.	☐ A train allows small animals. There is no extra charge.
☐ A plane ticket to Grandma's costs $96.00.	☐ A train ticket to Grandma's costs $104.00.

Should Keisha take a plane or a train? Explain why.

_____

_____

All Aboard!

Follow the maze to get to the next town.
Watch out for the big rocks!

Create

Folded Paper Plane

Make and fly a paper airplane.

Follow the directions to make a paper airplane:

1. Cut out the pattern on page 275. Fold the paper in half lengthwise.

2. Fold the left corner down to the fold line. Crease it.

3. Fold the left side down again to the fold line. Crease it.

4. Fold the left side down again to the fold line. Crease it.

5. Repeat steps 1–4, to the other side of the paper.

6. Add tape to the top and bottom of the plane to secure it.

7. Decorate your plane. See how far your plane can fly!

1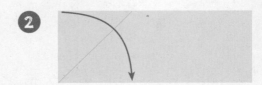

2

3 align

4 align

5

6 tape 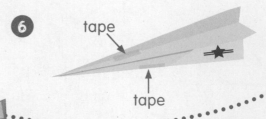 tape

Smart Start • EMC 9849 • © Evan-Moor Corp.

fold

fold

Thinking Skills

_____
Name

I **learned** that looking at things carefully, problem solving, and creating are critical thinking skills that I have.

I **did** activities that helped me think about my thinking so I can learn more and do more!

_____
Date

You Completed the Section
GOOD WORK!

ART

Tips

‣ Keep your child's supplies in a container so that everything is close at hand.

‣ Explain directions before your child begins a new type of activity.

‣ Show your child how the illustrations help show what to do.

‣ Encourage your child to pick up and throw away all scraps when a project is finished.

Supplies

‣ scissors

‣ glue stick or paste

‣ crayons or colored pencils

‣ marking pens

‣ pencil

‣ clear tape

‣ some projects may require additional supplies

Origami in the Fishbowl

1. Pull out page 281. Cut out the shapes.

2. Fold the paper shapes to make two fish.

3. Glue the tail on each fish.

4. Glue the sea grass, the little house, and the fish in the fishbowl on page 283.

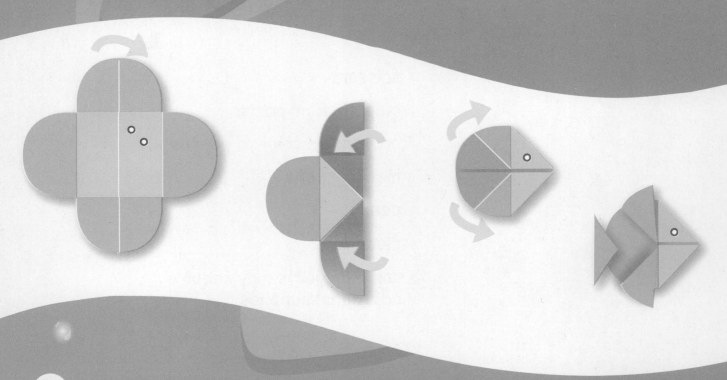

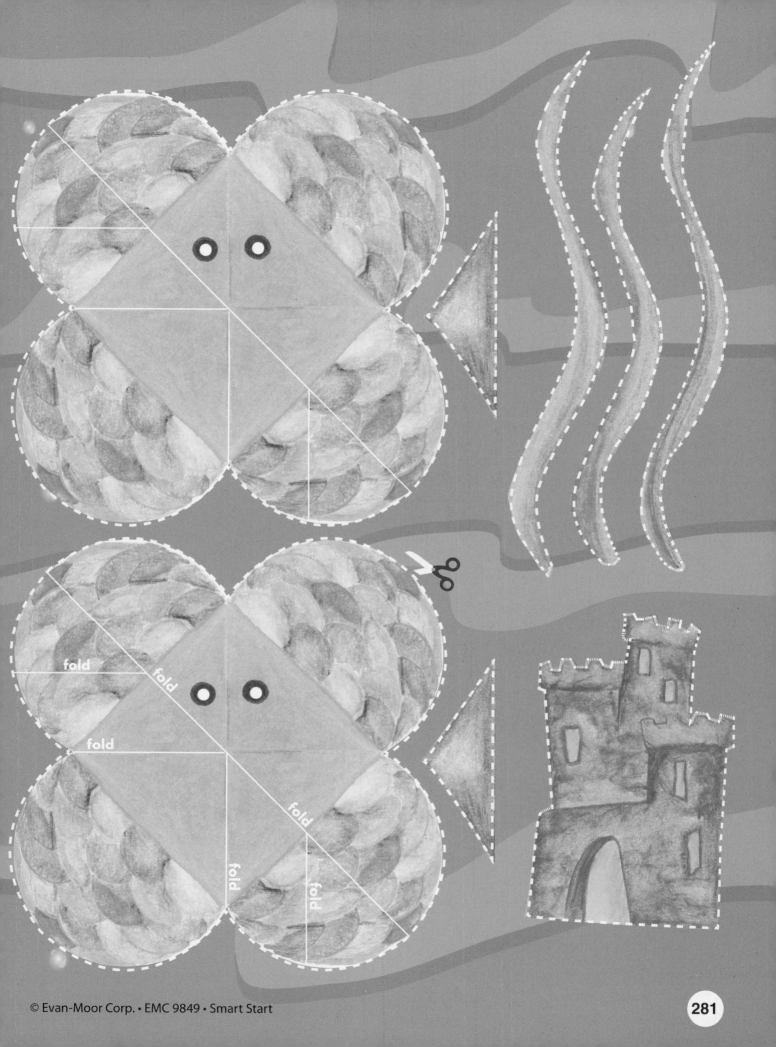

fold fold fold fold fold

Leo, the Loooong Dog

1. Cut out the dog parts.
2. Fold the middle part.
3. Glue the parts together.

Smart Start • EMC 9849 • © Evan-Moor Corp.

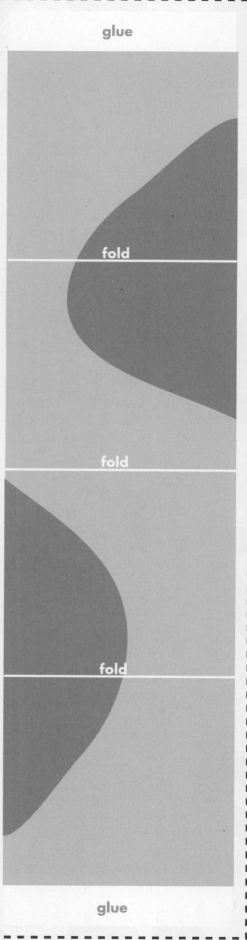

Word Search

Find the words from the word box in the word search.

```
c l o w n d m f
t r i c k o c u
s m i l e g l n
h t e n t c o n
a r i d e a w y
t n o s e r n z
u p c i r c u s
s c l o w n r t
```

Word Box

car	clown	funny	smile	trick
circus	dog	hat	tent	

How many times did you find the word clown? ⬤

© Evan-Moor Corp. • EMC 9849 • Smart Start

The Three Bears

A Pop-up Book

1. Cut out the patterns.

2. Make the pop-up book.

3. Glue the bears to the tabs.

4. Open and close the holder as you tell the story of The Three Bears and that naughty little Goldilocks.

cut fold cut

cut fold cut

The Three Bears

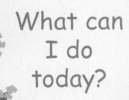

What can I do today?

A Hungry Bear

Count by 2s to connect the dots.

Draw Bears

Practice drawing a bear.

Smart Start • EMC 9849 • © Evan-Moor Corp.

Now make your bear dance and play.

Space Friends

1. Cut out the patterns.

2. Fold on the lines.

3. Glue as shown.
   After the glue dries, put one puppet on each hand.
   Let them tell each other about their home planets.

Smart Start • EMC 9849 • © Evan-Moor Corp.

Trouble in Space

List 8 things in this picture that don't make sense.

1. _____
2. _____
3. _____
4. _____

5. _____
6. _____
7. _____
8. _____

Feed the Frog

Make the Frog

1. Cut out the pattern.
2. Fold on the lines.
3. Pull out the pocket. Tape it.
4. Cross the legs. Tape them.

Make the Flies

1. Cut out the patterns.
2. Glue the flies to beans or buttons. Let the glue dry.

Feed the Frog

Toss the flies into the frog's pocket. How far away can you sit and still feed the frog?

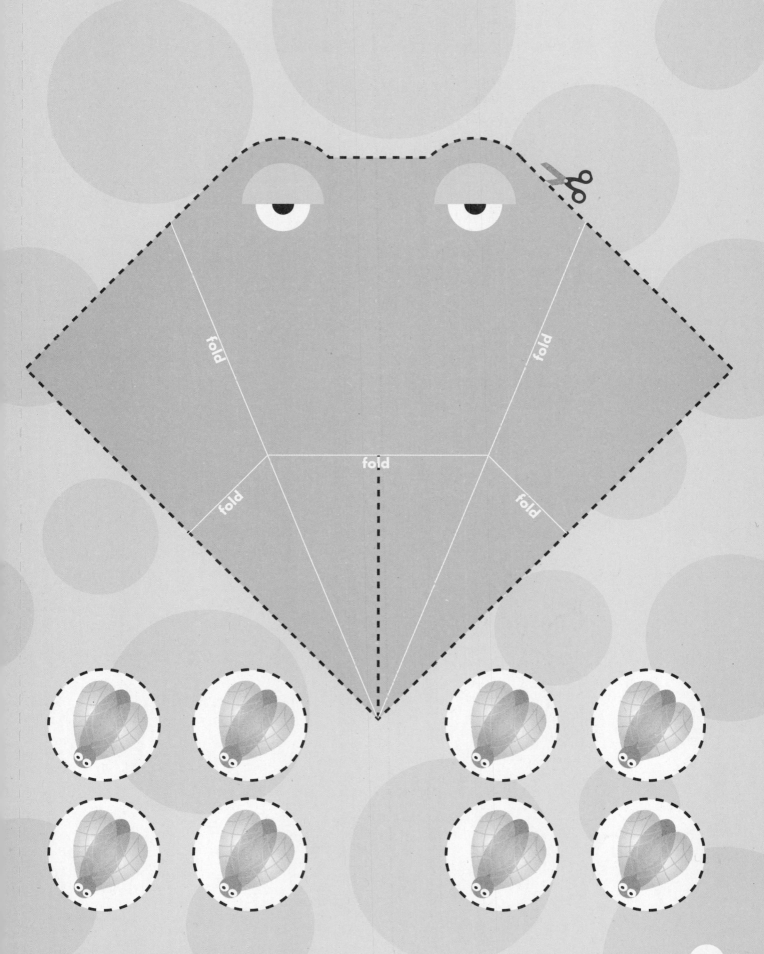

Smart Start • EMC 9849 • © Evan-Moor Corp.